WILD
FRANCE

WILD FRANCE

The Animals, Plants and Landscapes

BOB GIBBONS

First published in 2009 by New Holland Publishers (UK) Ltd
London • Cape Town • Sydney • Auckland

www.newhollandpublishers.com

Garfield House, 86–88 Edgware Road, London W2 2EA,
United Kingdom
80 McKenzie Street, Cape Town 8001, South Africa
Unit 1, 66 Gibbes Street, Chatswood, New South Wales,
Australia 2067
218 Lake Road, Northcote, Auckland, New Zealand

10 9 8 7 6 5 4 3 2 1

ISBN 978 1 84773 340 5

Senior Editor: Krystyna Mayer
Design: Alan Marshall
Cartographer: Stephen Dew
Production: Melanie Dowland
Commissioning Editor: Simon Papps
Editorial Direction: Rosemary Wilkinson

COVER AND PRELIMINARY PAGES
Front Cover: Herd of Ibex in the high Alps.
Back Cover: Purple Heron in the Camargue.
Page 1: Glanville Fritillary on Lady Orchid.
Page 2: Flowers including Purple Orchids, in pastures.
Page 3: Gryphon Vulture in flight on Col de Deux, Vercors.
Page 4: Male Ibex in the Alps.
Page 6, left: Mont St Michel; right: Little Owl.
Page 7, left: alpine rock garden; right: autumn countryside in
the mountains.

Reproduction by Pica Digital (Pte) Ltd, Singapore
Printed and bound in Singapore by Tien Wah Press

CONTENTS

INTRODUCTION

What an extraordinary country France is. It is the largest country lying wholly within Europe, contains part of the highest mountain in Europe, is the most visited country in the world (with 79 million visitors per year excluding day visitors), and borders eight other countries and two quite different seas. The coastline stretches for at least 5,500 km, the highest point is at Mont Blanc (4,808 m) and in between there are huge areas of semi-natural habitats at all elevations. However, these bald facts fail to reveal France's wonderful diversity and history, special architecture and fascinating wildlife, let alone its food, wine and culture. It is little wonder that France affords a continuing source of interest to those who live outside its boundaries.

LEFT Autumn view of the Mandailles Valley in the Volcans d'Auvergne Regional Natural Park.

METROPOLITAN FRANCE (THAT IS, THE MAINLAND plus Corsica and all the other nearby islands, but excluding all the Overseas Territories) covers an area of between 543,965 sq km (a figure that excludes all significant areas of open water, glaciers and estuaries) and 551,695 sq km (which includes all these). The latest figures show that 62 million people live in metropolitan France.

There is an interesting comparison to be drawn with Britain, where approximately 60 million people live in an area of 245,000 sq km – in other words, there is roughly 2.25 times as much land per person in France. Because of this extra space, land and property are cheaper, and there is a more relaxed view of the land. Many rural areas lie far from major population centres – much too far to commute – so communities are more self-sufficient and more deeply invested in the land than in more populous countries. This translates into a high degree of care for the landscape, especially in the southern two-thirds of the country, and profit is rarely the only motive for land management. Consequently, there is more traditional management of pastures and hay meadows, more deciduous broadleaved woodland and a better sense of the needs of the other denizens of the countryside than there is in most of the industrialized countries of Western Europe. In an ecological sense, France is at the crossroads of Europe, sharing species from virtually all the climatic zones of the Continent, as well as having a few of its own. It is also at the hub of the European migration wheel, and huge numbers of birds that do not actually breed in France pass through on their way to or from their breeding grounds.

This combination of position, size, habitat extent, varied geology and good climate has given France an exceptional variety of flora and fauna, as described in the following chapters.

The Geography

Although France often feels like a mountainous country, a glance at a relief map or satellite image quickly reveals how little of it is actually under high mountains. The northern third of France, lying roughly north of a line between Mulhouse and Nantes, is mainly low-lying, with the exception of the Ardennes along the Belgian border and the Vosges in the far north-east. Almost all of this area, apart from Brittany, lies over soft sedimentary rocks – in fact, this is the case with the whole

CLOCKWISE FROM THE TOP, LEFT A male Capercaillie on its breeding ground; a new-born Grey Seal pup on the north coast; Common Frogs in the breeding season, resting among duckweed; Black-veined Whites gathered on damp ground in the Maritime Alps.

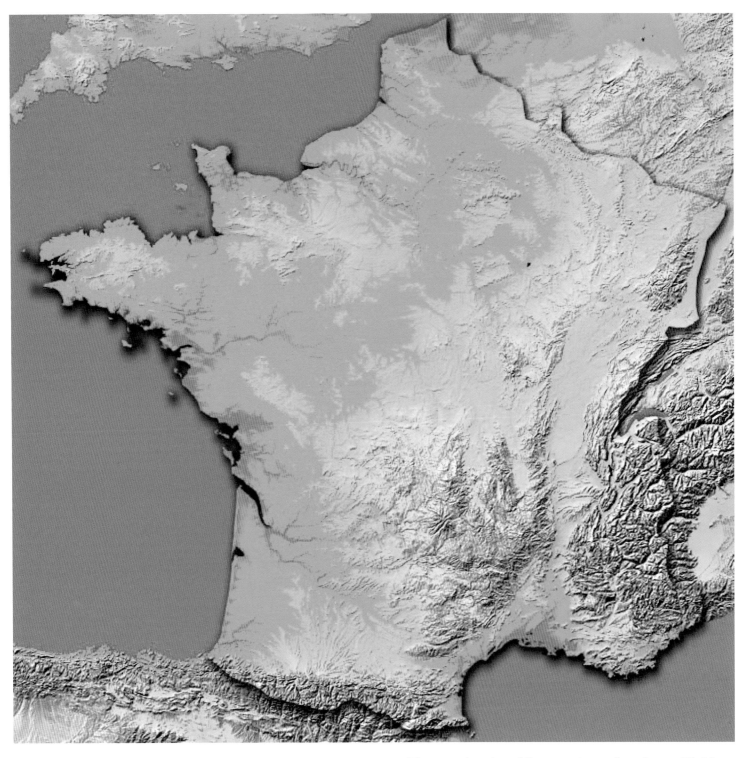

The Physical Geography of France

This extraordinary composite satellite photograph of mainland France, with the international boundaries added, clearly reveals the physical geography of the country.

It is obvious that the north and west are essentially lowland, and that the major rivers, apart from the Rhône, almost all drain westwards into the Atlantic and the English Channel. The main visible westwards-flowing rivers are, from north to south, the Seine, Loire and Garonne-Dordogne complex, merging to form the Gironde north of Bordeaux. Between them, these rivers drain most of the country. In the south, the Rhône is the only major river, cutting a deep valley between the Alps and the Massif Central – both clearly visible – to meet the Mediterranean just west of Marseille. Here, its vast flat delta can be clearly seen, though only parts remain in a natural condition, mostly within the Camargue Natural Regional Park.

The mountain regions of France stand out well on the map. The Vosges are a clearly defined block in the north-eastern corner, close to, although distinctly separated from, the limestone Jura that straddle the Franco–Swiss border for much of its length. The far south-east of France is dominated by the Alps, of which a substantial area lies in France, though this also gives a good idea of how big an arc of mountains the Alps are.

West of the Alps, the mountains are less high and less dominant, though the Vercors stand out as a clear north–south block of high land. The broad diffuse nature of the Massif Central can be clearly seen, and you can also distinguish the volcanic areas from the radial drainage pattern that can be easily seen in the north-west of the area. Finally, the dominant and significant role of the Pyrenees can be readily appreciated – they run across the neck of the Iberian Peninsula like an enormous wall, separating two cultures and ecological zones.

of the huge area known as the Parisian Basin, which overlies limestones, sandstones and other sedimentary rocks from the Jurassic, Cretaceous and later periods. It gives rise to a gently rolling countryside that is easily worked agriculturally, and is the most intensively farmed part of the country. The wide open plains of Champagne country and elsewhere are not of much appeal to the naturalist, especially as even hedges and trees are often absent, though fortunately such countryside is largely confined to this region. Where the sedimentary rocks meet the coast between the Belgian border and Cherbourg, there are either soft, low-lying coasts of dunes and marshes, or high, sheer chalk cliffs such as those at Etretat.

As you proceed westwards, especially west of a line between Caen and Angers, the character of the countryside changes. It becomes more Atlantic in nature, but the main difference lies in the rocks. Almost all of the rocks underlying Brittany are either hard ancient sedimentary rocks from the Cambrian, Pre-Cambrian or Ordovician Eras, or hard crystalline rocks of plutonic origin (rocks that were intruded as molten material into pre-existing rocks, but did not reach the surface at the time), such as granite. It is a hillier, harsher landscape, with more uncultivated areas and less intensive agriculture. Where the hard rocks meet the coast, they give rise to a classic drowned valley landscape – the pre-existing valley landforms have not been moulded significantly by the seas rising since the last ice age and have kept their valley shapes. The Breton coast is a spectacular one, with many headlands and cliffs, often separated by small coves and beaches. This whole area is known as the Massif Armoricain.

Southwards from the Nantes area right down to the border with Spain, the character of the west coast changes again, to a

RIGHT This picture shows a piece of beautiful French countryside, just south-west of Mont Louis in the Pyrenees, in autumn. Although it is not quite typical French countryside, it is nevertheless characteristic in the sense that it is varied, unspoiled and rich in wildlife and history.

The view shows part of the Eyne Plateau at about 1,600 m, just west of the village of Eyne. This is an area that has been strongly shaped by pastoral traditions that are now declining. In the foreground there is an old drove road edged on the left with an ancient granite wall showing signs of dereliction, while on the right the passage of endless hooves and feet has cut down through the sandy soil to produce a dry, south-facing bank, now rich in special flowers and warmth-loving insects. As often happens, the drove road is now used as a public footpath.

The pastures all around are still grazed, though not heavily, and most of the trees visible nearby are birches, which tend to readily invade neglected pasture and are indicative of reduced grazing pressures. Typically of mountain France, the pastures have not been agriculturally improved by fertilizers or ploughing, and remain full of flowers and other species.

Because of the layout of the mountains around the site (visible in the background), this is a particularly important site for southwards-migrating birds in autumn. It is well visited by birdwatchers, and in recent years has also started to become important for skiing.

ABOVE Ancient Corsican Pines growing as open forest high on the Col de Bavella, on the island of Corsica.

flatter, sandier landscape, without drowned valleys and cliffs. This is the Bassin Aquitain, a vast, low-lying area underlain by recent soft sediments (geologically recent, that is), and drained westwards by the Garonne River and its tributaries. At its south-eastern tip, this region reaches across to beyond Toulouse, almost to the Mediterranean, bounded to the south by the Pyrenees, and to the north and east by the great Massif Central.

The Massif Central dominates central southern France, running northwards from Toulouse almost to Dijon, and from the Rhône Valley to west of Limoges. This is no simple mountain range – it is a highly complex block of hills and mountains, a convoluted mass of volcanic, plutonic, sedimentary and meta-morphic rocks, with an extraordinary variety of scenery and a flora and fauna to match. Perhaps surprisingly, its name is of only recent origin, from a 19th-century literary work, though the names of its components, such as the Auvergne and Cévennes, go back much further.

The Pyrenees are easily defined. They form a huge wall that runs across the whole neck of the Iberian Peninsula, where France and Spain meet, pushed up by the collision of two great land masses. They are not simple geologically, but their role as an ecological, climatic and social barrier is unequivocal (see Chapter 2).

The whole eastern boundary of France is dominated by an unbroken line of mountains, from the Vosges in the north to the Maritime Alps in the south, described in more detail in Chapter 2. This combination of low-lying land in the west with moun-tains in the east has given France a rather skewed watershed – the majority of the rivers drain westwards into the Atlantic, with hardly any running south or east, so that about 80 per cent of the country drains into the Atlantic Ocean.

The remaining southern part of the mainland is defined as the Provence geological region, squeezed between the Pyrenees, Massif Central and Alps, running northwards up the great north–south trench that is the Rhône Valley. This is a warm and welcoming landscape, gentle in places, and under-lain almost entirely by sedimentary rocks that are mainly lime-stone, except for the odd outcrop of granite and other rocks in the Massif des Maures. There are many hills and even a few mountains; all are of light-coloured, barely forested lime-stones, and none reaches any great height.

The tour of France ends at Corsica, the 'range of mountains in the sea'. This 8,680-sq km island lies well off the French coast, about 160 km at the nearest point, and is undeniably a world apart in almost every respect. It is indeed very mountainous, with peaks all through it, reaching their highest point at Monte Cinto (2,706 m), and including many other peaks of more than 2,000 m. The bulk of the land is made up of plutonic rocks, especially granite but including ophiolites (sections of the Earth's oceanic crust and upper mantle that have been uplifted) and others. Small areas lie over sedimentary rocks, of which the most significant is the beautiful area around Bonifacio, at the southern tip, which lies on a white, chalk-like Miocene limestone, and has a very different flora from the rest of the island. The combination of rugged high topography and hard acidic rock has left Corsica remarkably unspoiled, with limited agricultural and tourism-related developments, and vast areas of forests and almost inaccessible peaks.

The Climate

The climate of France is temperate and mild but, as in so many other ways, France lies at something of a crossroads in its climatic patterns, influenced by three major climatic zones. These are the Atlantic, Continental and Mediterranean zones – of which the Atlantic is the most significant – and they are combined with the locally generated climates of the higher mountain systems. There is no straightforward and simple division into zones, but rather a dynamic and shifting pattern as the climatic zones meet and influence each other and additionally, of course, the pattern is currently changing due to the uncertain effects of global warming. The Atlantic affects the whole of the country to a certain degree, partly because it is such a powerful force, generating strong westerly winds that move across the country, often as part of major depression systems that may sweep on far beyond the eastern boundaries of France. Its effects are also strengthened by France's topography, since the lack of high ground over most of the west and north fails to interrupt the passage of the winds and their moisture.

All the western lowland areas have broadly similar climates, with mild winters and only moderately hot summers, though there is a gradation both southwards and eastwards to hotter summers. Rainfall is generally quite heavy (80–100 cm a year), spread throughout the year in the more northern parts, but increasingly more seasonal towards the south, and tending to fall in shorter, heavier bursts. The winter temperatures on the west coast are among the warmest in France, with the average

BELOW An ancient beech forest high up in the French Pyrenees on a misty autumn day.

ABOVE January hoar frost accumulated on birches in a peat bog near Morez in the Jura Mountains.

minimum for the coldest month lying between 4 and 8°C. As you move eastwards through the low-lying areas of the Paris basin, north of the Massif Central, the effect of the Atlantic steadily diminishes – winters are progressively colder, and summers are hotter. In the flat areas, rainfall also gradually decreases eastwards, until the rising land of the Jura or Vosges intervenes. The western slopes of these mountains, especially the Vosges where the topography is more clear cut, are very wet, taking whatever rain is left in the Atlantic depressions.

The easternmost parts of France are the most continental in character, though because virtually the whole of the east is mountainous, this introduces many local complications. The Rhine Valley around Colmar has the most continental climate in France, partly because it is far to the east, but also because it is in the rain shadow of the Vosges – Colmar is the driest large town in France, with an average annual rainfall of 53 cm per year, compared with the national average of 77 cm per

year. Higher parts of this same general area have extremely cold winters – the lowest recorded temperature of anywhere inhabited in France was in the Jura near Morez, at -41°C. The local effects of mountains on climates are discussed in more detail in Chapter 2.

The Massif Central is something of an oddity, climatically, because of its position. Its western faces present the first high ground to the east of the Atlantic, and as such they receive very heavy rainfall and are rather strongly Atlantic in character (though overlain by the cooling effects of altitude). The eastern side of the Massif is much more continental in character, with lower rainfall, hotter summers and colder winters. On the south side, where the high limestone *causses* run down towards the Mediterranean coast, the climate is warm and Mediterranean in character.

The southern part of France, south of the Massif Central and between the Pyrenees and Maritime Alps, has a rather specific climate. The Mediterranean climate is distinct enough to have been used to describe the climates of a number of regions elsewhere in the world. It is characterized by hot, dry summers and

mild winters, and most of the rainfall is spread through the period between autumn and spring. Levels of rainfall are actually quite high, sometimes higher than the national average, but the pattern of rainfall is quite different. For example, Nice has an average rainfall of 76.7 cm per year, compared with the national average of 77 cm, but very little of the rain falls in summer, and in general the Mediterranean areas have fewer rainy days than the rest of the country, averaging around 60 cm per year. Average temperatures of the coolest month vary between 6 and 10°C, slightly warmer than the Atlantic coasts, but summers are much hotter.

The effect of this pattern of weather on the vegetation is considerable, as plants have to adapt to a long period of hot, dry weather, and this different character of the vegetation is immediately obvious as soon as you visit the area. It is described in more detail in Chapter 4.

One feature of the climate of southern France that is not specifically associated with a Mediterranean climate, but rather with its position relative to the high mountains, is the seasonal winds. The best known of these are the Mistral of

ABOVE The Gorge de la Vis, one of the many limestone gorges cutting through the southern Massif Central.
OVERLEAF A spectacular alpine lake on the Col du Joly, covered with floating bur-reed.

Provence and the Tramontane of Languedoc. These are strong, often violent winds from the north that in the worst areas may blow for well over a hundred days a year. They are katabatic winds, caused by air cooling over the mountains (especially the Alps and Massif Central).

As cool air is denser than warm air, it falls, and because of the peculiar topography of the Rhône Valley, this cool air steadily collects in the valley – very like the waters of all the tributaries coming down into the Rhône – from where it is funnelled down towards the coast at increasing speed. The effect is exacerbated as the warm air in the south is tending to rise, creating a vacuum that pulls in the cold air from the mountains. These seasonal winds can go on for such a long period of time that they are said to drive people completely mad in bad years.

Chapter I

THE LOWLAND HABITATS OF FRANCE

Despite the extent and effects of France's successful agricultural industry, the lowlands of France still support a wonderful range of almost natural habitats. Forests are the dominant feature, covering well over a quarter of the land surface, but there are also some huge wetland areas, many flowery lowlands, grasslands and heathland, and vast areas of those particularly French-sounding habitats, *garrigue* and *maquis*. Although often more fragmented and affected by farming and development than mountain areas (see Chapter 2), these lowland habitats are especially rich in species, particularly when they cover large areas of land.

LEFT Roadside flowers including Viper's Bugloss, Yellow Rattle and Cow-wheat on the limestone plateau north of Dijon.

Forests, wetland areas, flowery lowlands, grasslands, heathlands, *garrigue* and *maquis* – all rich in flora and fauna – comprise the lowland habitats of France.

ABOVE Forests and pasture in the Auvergne near Murol in late autumn, after an early snowfall.

The Forests

France's forests are among its greatest treasures. Almost anywhere that you go in France, there is forest close to you, and they play an enormous part in French rural life, much more than in most other industrialized countries. This is partly because the forest cover here is very high – estimated at 28.2 per cent of the land surface in the 2005 inventory, covering about 155,000 sq km of terrain. It therefore comes as little surprise that you are never far from a significant area of woodland (with a few notable regional exceptions, such as parts of Champagne and Brittany). However, the human inhabitants' intimate association with, and love of, woodland goes back much further in history, and it is here that most of the clues to the biological richness of French forests lie.

In common with most northern temperate countries, France has been affected in relatively recent times by four major ice ages, the last of which ended around 15,000 years ago (depending on which part of France you have in mind, and how exactly you define 'ended'). At their height, huge ice sheets stretched southwards to northern France and outwards from major mountain areas, scouring the ground and leaving much of the land bare of vegetation – an ecological clean sheet. The effects were most marked, of course, in the north

and at higher altitudes, but tundra vegetation stretched as far south as Bordeaux, so the effects were very widespread. On mainland France, at least, there would have been virtually no true forest at the height of the last ice age.

As the climate warmed up again, so the forest began to recolonize. France has direct connections with warmer unglaciated lands southwards in present-day Spain and Italy, where forest survived (unlike in Britain and Ireland, where recolonization was inhibited as they became isolated by rising sea levels), and the passage northwards and upwards of the forest edge was relatively fast. By about 7000–6000 BC, forest covered most of the land available to it – that is to say, land below the prevailing altitudinal tree-line, wherever conditions were suitable, though there is still discussion among ecologists as to how dense the forest cover actually was. It is hard to believe, now, that the extensive open *garrigue* of France, and the vast open limestone pastures of the *causses*, were forested not so long ago, but all the available evidence indicates that they were, and that it is almost entirely human influence that has caused this change.

From this peak of forest cover, there followed a steady though fluctuating decline for thousands of years, beginning with the Neolithic Revolution, as settled agriculture and clearance of the forest flourished, so that by the dawn of the Christian era only about half of the land surface was wooded.

This continued through the Roman and Gallo-Roman eras and the steady population expansion in the Middle Ages. During this period, a changing climate contributed to the retreat.

Since the 14th century, however, the pattern has been more variable and less clear. The great plagues of the mid-14th century and the ravages of the 100 Years War (1337–1453) brought about many changes, including an estimated 66 per cent drop in the population. This led to much of the agricultural land being abandoned and thus becoming available for recolonization by woodland. A temporary rise in woodland area at this period was soon followed by further declines as the population rose again, and new uses for timber were found in the industrial and pre-industrial eras.

In 1661, following a period of concern about the future of forests (royal forests in particular), Jean Baptiste Colbert, in his role as superintendent of finances, signed an order for the enclosure and regulation of all the royal forests, which set in motion a period of detailed examination of forest management, boundaries and practices. Soon after, in 1669, an Ordinance was signed that was to regulate the management of forests for the next 150 years. There was, however, no immediate effect on

ABOVE Lying at 800–2,600 m, the densely forested Massif des Maures near La Garde-Freinet is distinctly mountainous.

BELOW The vast grasslands on the limestone *causses* of southern France were well wooded before the advent of man.

forest area, and by the beginning of the 19th century forest cover had reached its post-glacial nadir of about 75,000 sq km (about 13.5 per cent of the land surface). Since then, it has risen steadily to today's figure, due to depopulation of rural

ABOVE Silver Birches recolonizing old heathland in the Sologne, now that grazing has ceased here.

areas and a vast, albeit episodic programme of reforestation carried out largely by the state. The Forest Code of 1827 led to a flurry of planting, notably in Les Landes de Gascogne (which ultimately led to the forming of Western Europe's largest forest in a vast triangle lying south of Bordeaux), the Sologne, Champagne and many mountain areas.

Even at its lowest ebb, the forest area in France covered a higher proportion of the land than the modern-day forest areas do in Britain, Holland, Belgium, Denmark, Ireland and some other European nations. It is hardly surprising that it plays such an important role in France's culture.

It has been said that 'place names are the fossils of human geography', and it is interesting to look at the names of forests and settlements in France. Words for forest or woodland are legion here, with many different derivations from Latin, Basque, Catalan, German, Breton and so on. Words such as *bois, buc* and *bosquet* are common and obvious enough, but *breuil* comes from an old Gallic name for a woodland sur-

rounded by a wall; *gaut* or *gault* comes from the Germanic *wald* meaning forest, *gayon* comes from the Basque, *vabre* comes from the Langue D'oc and *jeux* comes from Franco-Provencal dialect.

Although such names often refer to currently wooded sites, they can also give clues to formerly wooded areas. Other words give more information on the past history or vegetation of a forest; for example, *fage, hagedo, fayolle, futelaie, faouet, foys* and many others all indicate the presence of woodland dominated by beech (with some of the names bearing a clear resemblance to the scientific name of Common Beech, *Fagus sylvatica*). The names *Cernay* (of which there are many) and *Cerneux*, including the intriguing *Noël-Cerneux*, all refer to the practice of ring-barking (*cerner* in French) by which early clearances may have taken place, and the word *essart* or *assart* (denoting wholesale clearance of woodland) contributes the root of many place names.

When you travel around France, you will frequently see signs saying *forêt domaniale* or *forêt communale* as you enter a forest. The *forêt domaniales* are forests owned by the state, and they make up about 10 per cent of the whole forest area, with a total of about 1,500 distinct forests. Most commonly, such forests are direct descendants of former royal, monastic or signorial forests that were seized at the time of the French Revolution (1789–99), and their modern-day distribution tends to reflect this (though there are also many more modern state forests, with a much shorter history). They are particularly common in the Ile de France, Normandie, the Cévennes and the southern Alps, with lesser numbers in Lorraine and Champagne-Ardenne, while in other areas they are virtually absent. Such forests are all managed directly by the Office National des Forêts (ONF) under the legal framework provided since their establishment in 1966.

Forêts communales are distinctly different in their history. They are forests that are owned by a *commune* (usually), department or region, and their origins as part of village life generally stretch back well into the Middle Ages. Whatever their original ownership, such forests gradually accrued to the community as common rights of wood, grazing, pannage (the right to put out pigs in autumn to eat the acorns) and others became more established and the power of the gentry or royalty waned. Some communal forests derive from replanted communal agricultural land, but most of them are genuinely ancient forests with a continuous history of woodland since the Ice Age retreated.

Nowadays, the area of communal forests covers roughly 2.5 million ha, and comprises 17 per cent of the national forest area, although the distribution of communal forests is heavily skewed towards the east and south of France, and is particularly strong in mountain areas. Out of the 36,000 communities in France, about 11,000 are forest owners, and are known as *communes forestières*. In general, communal forests do not look so very different from state ones, and although strategic

decisions about them are made by the communities, they are usually managed on their behalf by the ONF.

For the naturalist, it is usually these two types of publicly owned forest that are of most interest. They are frequently large and of ancient origin, and still retain a semblance of native vegetation, albeit often in a highly modified form. Also, the defined forest area frequently includes a variety of other semi-natural habitats of interest, including grasslands, heathland, open water, wetlands and scrub, and their presence within the forest matrix makes for an environment that is richer than the sum of its parts – isolated blocks of a single habitat are generally much poorer in species.

In addition, access is usually welcome, though it should be remembered that these forests only make up a little over a quarter of the area of forest cover – the rest is in private hands, split between several million owners. A large native deciduous forest in France probably supports about 6,000 species of animal, of which about 75 per cent are insects, and such places are literally buzzing with activity in high summer.

In general, the management of French forests is wildlife friendly, following principles of selective removal of mature trees and the use of natural regeneration rather than the clear-felling and monoculture replanting so favoured in some other countries, though of course there are many exceptions. This does not mean that the remaining forest vegetation is what would be there naturally, but it does mean that there has usually been a continuity of the woodland environment and many of the key species within it, which is so important to the survival of the biodiversity of woodland.

Most forests have been managed to a greater or lesser degree, and this always changes the balance of the dominant species, even if only in subtle ways. Particularly palatable trees, such as the limes (*Tilia* spp.), often steadily decline as, once cut down, their regrowth is too desirable to browsing animals (wild or domestic), and they fail to maintain their place in the canopy. The large oaks (Common Oak, *Quercus robur*, and Sessile Oak, *Q. petraea*) were frequently favoured by monarchs such as Louis XIV, and regeneration areas were specifically set aside for them. Interestingly, though, this has sometimes led to an

ABOVE The Forest of Cerisy, near Bayeux, is a fine example of a mixed beech and oak forest, managed as a nature reserve.

increase in the Common Beech (*Fagus sylvatica*) in more recent times as lack of management of the dense oak regeneration plots has led to a dark forest floor on which only beeches can regenerate. This is particularly noticeable in parts of Fontainebleau Forest, south of Paris. Most other trees have waxed and waned according to whims of the period.

The native tree flora of European forests is generally rather poor compared to that of other regions, especially tropical ones, due partly to the effects of recent glaciations. The tree flora of France is richer than average for Europe, though, because of its large areas of primary woodland (areas with continuous woodland cover since the post-Ice Age forest), wide range of geological and physical conditions, and position at the meeting place of three climatic zones (see Introduction). It has a much higher proportion of broadleaved trees than most other European countries, at about two-thirds of the forested area (and most of the dominant broadleaves are native species), and many of its coniferous forests are made up of native coniferous trees such as the European Larch (*Larix decid-*

uas), Norway Spruce (*Picea abies*) and Silver Fir (*Abies alba*) growing in their natural environment in mountain areas.

Oaks

Oaks are the most common dominant trees – an oak species is the primary tree in well over a quarter of French forests (the Sessile Oak in 12 per cent, Common Oak in 11 per cent and Downy Oak, *Quercus pubescens*, in 4 per cent). However, it should always be remembered that the figures can be misleading, as they do not indicate that these trees are the only tree species in such situations, and the accuracy of the data is not always wholly reliable.

Roughly speaking, the Common Oak is more common in the west and in the lowlands, while the Sessile Oak is more common in the east and in the uplands. The semi-evergreen Downy Oak (it holds its leaves through the winter, only losing them when new growth starts) tends to occur on calcareous soils in areas that are hot, but not too hot, such as the Dordogne or the area around Dijon. It is replaced in the hottest areas by the evergreen Holm Oak (*Quercus ilex*) or, on acidic soils, by the Cork Oak (*Q. suber*). The Holm Oak is widespread as a dominant or scattered tree in Mediterranean France, though the Cork Oak is rather rare, with pockets in the Massif des Albères (south-west France) and Massif des Maures (southeast France) – it is scarce elsewhere.

Beeches

The Common Beech plays a huge role in French forests, dominating at least 11 per cent of the woodland area. It is a tree that likes some summer warmth but not drought; in optimum conditions it is frequently virtually dominant. Beech forests are wonderful places, both visually and for their associated species, especially in the little-managed montane forests. Many lowland forests, such as Compiègne, are dominated by tall, stately beeches, though they lack the fascinating shapes and ecological niches of some of the highland beech forests. There are superb examples of ancient beech forests scattered through the Pyrenees, the Auvergne and many alpine areas such as the Massif des Bauges, the Vercors and Mont Ventoux.

In drier parts of France, the Common Beech becomes increasingly confined to the mountains and often to the damper northern slopes; in low-rainfall mountain areas such as Queyras and parts of the Maritime Alps, it is virtually absent at its normal altitudinal range. There is a fascinating isolated relict Common Beech woodland on north-facing slopes in the Massif de la Sainte Baume, just east of Marseille, now protected and managed for its special value, but generally the Common Beech is rare at lower altitudes of the Mediterranean area.

ABOVE The flowers and new foliage of beech bursting out in spring. BELOW Mixed open forest of Cork Oaks and other trees in the Massif des Maures, Provence.

Sweet Chestnuts

In parts of France, the Sweet Chestnut (*Castanea sativa*) is the dominant tree (it totals about 5 per cent of the forest area), in areas from the Massif Central southwards, where conditions are warm enough for it to fruit well. It grows perfectly well much further north, but because its fruits are edible, the pro-

ductivity of its nuts becomes an important factor in determining where it has been encouraged. It is one of the trees that often comes to assume a key role in the economy of a community – it provides both small wood and large timber, and its fruits can be either eaten directly or converted into flour and other products. The Sweet Chestnut grows best on acid soils, so it is most common in areas such as the Massif des Maures, the southern Cévennes and the mountains of Corsica. Although frequently still important, its relative value has declined as so many more food products are available everywhere, and it is not uncommon now to see chestnuts rotting on the ground in vast quantities in autumn.

Conifers

Coniferous forest is rarely dear to the naturalist's heart – in Britain at least – although this is largely because of its association with dense plantations of usually non-native conifers. Well-managed or unmanaged ancient coniferous woods are another matter, both beautiful and rich in life. As a general rule, they dominate in cooler mountain areas, where they are well adapted to the difficulties of mountain life. The Norway Spruce (*Picea abies*) and Silver Fir (*Abies amabilis*) both form beautiful forests in many of France's damper forest areas, especially the Vosges, Jura, more northerly Alps and Pyrenees. Generally, the Norway Spruce is the hardier, continuing to higher altitudes, and the Silver Fir is more common in the more southerly Pyrenees, though they both dominate roughly the same percentage of forest.

Ancient spruce and fir forests have a rich ground flora, and other forms of life are abundant. In drier areas, both tend to be replaced by the European Larch, which is dominant in many of the southern alpine areas, such as Queyras, Massif des Ecrins and the appropriately named Col de Larche, forming beautiful stands that turn a rich orange in autumn before the needles drop. Because of the tree's deciduous nature and its occurrence in steep mountain areas where management is limited, the ground flora and general fauna can be very abundant, combining woodland and grassland species.

At the highest altitudes other conifers increasingly appear, including the Arolla Pine (*Pinus cembra*), the similar Mountain Pine (*P. uncinata*) and the Dwarf Pine (*P. mugo*), though these trees rarely form forests on their own. In warmer areas, especially on limestone, the Scots Pine (*P. silvestris*) can form extensive and attractive open forests, while the Aleppo Pine (*P. halepensis*) is a common transition forest tree, invading cleared areas, abandoned terraces and so on in the Mediterranean area. In Corsica, the dominant conifer in the higher mountain areas is the Corsican Pine (*Pinus nigra* subsp. *salzmannii* var. *corsicana*), unpopular when planted in dense plantations in Britain, but a wonderful species in its native habitat.

RIGHT Autumn view of part of the vast extent of European Larch forest that clothes the slopes of the Queyras Natural Regional Park.

Flora and Fauna

Whatever the dominant trees are, the old forests of France are wonderful places for nature and the naturalist. They are *the* place for fungi, with far more species occurring in woodlands than anywhere else, including many of the finest edible ones such as the boletes. The high humidity of large woodlands allows mosses and liverworts to flourish, especially in Atlantic and montane regions, and also lichens, broadly speaking. The woodland flora is huge, and the less intensively managed forests, especially on limestone, are a delight, filled with orchids, Bastard Balm (*Melittis melissophyllum*), Solomon's seal (*Polygonatum* spp.), Lily-of-the-Valley (*Convallaria majalis*), Martagon Lily (*Lilium martagon*), ferns, club mosses and many others.

Birds are here in abundance, of course, varying according to the structure and position of the woodland. The list includes the Redstart (*Phoenicurus phoenicurus*), Blackcap (*Sylvia atricapilla*), Wood Warbler (*Phylloscopus sibilatrix*), Pied Flycatcher (*Ficedula hypoleuca*), Crossbill (*Loxia curvirostra*), all of the woodpeckers including the impressive Black Woodpecker (*Dryocopus martius*), several owls, and rarities such as the Capercaillie (*Tetrao urogallus*), now confined to rather few woodland areas in the eastern mountains.

The woodlands are the last refuge of a large number of mammals, and it is only in large woodland blocks that many larger animals can survive. The Brown Bear (*Ursus arctos*) is an exceptional case, subject to much controversy (see page 114), confined in France to just a few wooded areas in the Pyrenees. The Western Polecat (*Mustela putorius*), Pine Marten (*Martes martes*) and Beech Marten (*M. foina*) are all essentially forest animals, which are widespread in France. The Eurasian Lynx (*Lynx lynx*) and Wildcat (*Felis silvestris*) are both rare animals in France, mainly confined to eastern mountain areas, always associated with woodland.

Most of the large herbivores such as deer, the Chamois (*Rupicapra rupicapra*) and even the Ibex (*Capra ibex*) use forests for feeding and shelter, especially in winter, while two other classic woodland mammals occurring throughout France are the Red Squirrel (*Sciurus vulgaris*) and the more secretive Wild Boar (*Sus scrofa*).

While insects are not, perhaps, as obvious in forests as in flowery grasslands, the number of species is actually much higher, especially in mixed forests with ample clearings, rides and wet areas. Many species rely heavily on dead or dying wood for part of their lifecycle, including the longhorn beetles, cardinal beetles and many flies. Some butterflies are woodland specialists, or at least need an element of woodland within

TOP, LEFT The Pied Flycatcher breeds in hollows in deciduous and mixed forests in eastern France.

CENTRE, LEFT Wild Boar are a common, though secretive, mammal in rural France.

BOTTOM, LEFT Common Solomon's Seal in flower in woodland in spring.

their habitat area. These include several hairstreaks, the Purple Emperor (*Apatura iris*), White Admiral (*Limenitis camilla*) and Southern White Admiral (*L. reducta*), Large Tortoiseshell (*Nymphalis polychloros*), Silver-washed Fritillary (*Argynnis paphia*) and Speckled Wood (*Pararge aegeria*) among others, and many moths are essentially woodland species.

Some of the best examples of French forests are given in Chapter 9.

Scrub

Scrub is not exactly forest, but it does have many similarities. It refers to land dominated by shrubs, though there may be scattered trees or open areas within it. It is rarely a persistent habitat without some kind of intervention – almost invariably it is a transitional stage between open ground and woodland, although occasionally it remains unchanged for long periods where the conditions are too difficult for forest to develop readily. There is a small amount of natural climax scrub in mountain areas around the tree-line, covered in more detail in Chapter 2.

Scrub is a hard habitat to map, assess and define, though it is often fascinating to the naturalist, especially when it is not too

ABOVE A mass of Purging Broom growing on Mont Aigoual, Cévennes National Park, in the Languedoc-Roussillon region of southern France.

dense. For example, a belt of scrub around deciduous woodland, composed perhaps of the Blackthorn (*Prunus spinosa*), Hawthorn (*Crataegus monogyna*), Spindle (*Euonymus europaeus*) and other shrubs, makes a perfect habitat for butterflies, moths and other insects, breeding birds such as warblers and nightingales, and much else besides. Scrub within grassland immediately raises the number of invertebrates and birds, though there can be a problem in getting the right balance as scrub can invade the grassland and oust its specialist species.

The *Maquis*

Perhaps the best-known scrub habitat in France is the *maquis*, after which the famous wartime resistance movement was named. The *maquis* differs from the more open *garrigue* (see page 36) in that it consists of dense shrubs, usually of at least head height (thus supplying excellent cover for resistance groups!). Generally speaking, it is a secondary or degraded habitat, in the sense that it follows on from woodland clearance, invading abandoned agricultural land or *garrigue* on which grazing has ceased.

ABOVE The distinctive acorns and leaves of the Dwarf Oak, a key species growing in the *maquis*.

OPPOSITE A wonderful flowery hay meadow with Wild Daffodils below the Cirque de Gavarnie in the high Pyrenees.

BELOW A female Sardinian Warbler – the *maquis* bird par excellence – on the way to its nest.

The *Maquis* is a Mediterranean phenomenon, though it grades gradually into other more northerly scrub types. There is nothing essentially unusual about it, but it is so common in Mediterranean areas that it warrants a name. The dominant shrubs or small trees are commonly the Dwarf or Kermes Oak (*Quercus coccifera*), Strawberry Tree (*Arbutus unedo*), Myrtle (*Myrtus communis*), Rosemary (*Rosmarinus officinalis*) and brooms such as the Spiny Broom (*Calicotome villosa*). At its densest, it is almost impenetrable and poor in species, though a few, such as the Sardinian Warbler (*Sylvia melanocephala*), always seem to be there. Within France, it reaches its greatest extent in Corsica, especially in the northern part, though it is widespread on the mainland Mediterranean coast, too.

Open Habitats – Grasslands, Heathland and *Garrigue*

To be in a flowery pasture in summer or a beautiful stretch of coastal *garrigue* in spring is one of the greatest pleasures for the naturalist in France (unless you suffer from hay fever!). The colours, scents and mass of insect activity are almost overwhelming in their effect on the senses. Among Western European countries, France probably provides more opportunities for such pleasures than any other country – I say 'probably' because it is hard to get exact figures for the sort of habitats that concern us here. It is known, for example, that grasslands cover almost 30 per cent of France's land surface, but most of these grasslands are simply heavily fertilized monoculture dedicated to maximum agricultural productivity, and therefore of little relevance here. It is the herb-rich, flowery, often ancient grasslands, which have been managed with little ploughing or application of artificial fertilizer, that hold the wildlife. While there is no detailed assessment of their extent, they are still remarkably common and widespread in France, especially in the hills and mountain areas.

Grasslands, heathland and *garrigue* are all, with a few exceptions, artificial habitats in the sense that they have been created by the clearance of post-glacial forest by humans, followed by some means of keeping them tree-free, such as grazing, cutting or burning. On most soils, in moderately damp temperate climatic areas, grasslands result from clearance followed by grazing or mowing. Many of the most attractive flowery grasslands are of ancient origin, sometimes stretching back to their original clearance, and often hundreds of years old. The approximate age of a grassland is usually revealed by the number of species of flower in it, and to some extent, by the species composition. For example, dandelions (*Taraxacum* spp.), yellow rattles (*Rhinanthus* spp.), the Red Clover (*Trifolium pratense*), White Clover (*T. repens*), Yarrow (*Achillea millefolium*) and Common Ox-eye Daisy (*Leucanthemum vulgare*) all colonize grassland quite readily, whereas some orchids, scabiouses, gentians, saxifrages, Betony (*Stachys officinalis*) and others colonize only slowly.

Grasslands

Broadly speaking, flowery grasslands fall into two types: hay meadows, which are cut for hay once or more each year (though some may be grazed after the final cut of the year), and pastures, which are simply grazed by stock. They often have quite different species of both plant and animal. Hay meadows are usually on fertile soils, often damp and sometimes prone to winter flooding, whereas pastures usually occupy the sites unsuitable for vehicle access or too infertile to be worth it. Grazing produces an uneven sward (depending on the animals and the pattern of their grazing), with unpalatable species left alone, and many species are able to flower and seed if grazing is not too heavy. In hay meadows, the sudden truncation of

ABOVE A lovely hay meadow in the Dordogne at harvest time, dominated by Pyramidal Orchids and other uncommon species.

BELOW The White-winged Snowfinch is one of the most specialized of alpine birds, found at the highest altitudes.

growth stops numerous plants from seeding, and makes survival difficult for many insects if they cannot complete their lifecycle before the hay is cut. An isolated hay meadow generally has a rather limited butterfly and general insect fauna, though where there are many meadows together and edges or verges are often left uncut, diversity can be very rich.

One feature that frequently distinguishes old pastures is the presence of anthills. These are low humps up to about 50 cm high and perhaps a metre across, which are often abundant where they do occur. They are caused by Yellow Meadow Ants (*Lasius flavus*) and related species, and the bigger they are, the older they are. You can be pretty sure that a pasture with abundant anthills has been grassland for quite a while, because they are destroyed by ploughing, harrowing and over-shading.

Most of the best flowery grasslands are in the mountains and more hilly areas. Particularly good areas include the Auvergne, Pyrenees, Queyras Natural Regional Park, Massif des Bauges near Annecy (where there was a conference in 2007 specifically about the protection of flowery grasslands and their use in the agricultural system) and Haut Jura, as well as the vast limestone *causses* in the Cévennes area and much of the Dordogne. In the higher parts of these mountains, the grasslands come close to being natural pastures. The natural tree-lines can be roughly defined as 1,200–1,300 m in the Vosges, 1,300–1,500 m in the Jura and Massif Central, 1,800–2,000 m in the northern Alps and up to 2,400 m in the southern Alps and Pyrenees. These are the altitudes at which tree growth would cease under natural conditions, though in practice they are normally lower due to increased grazing by stock and a certain amount of clearance and fire, so that the area of alpine grassland is larger than it would be in the absence of man. Many of these mountain grasslands are still grazed by cattle and sheep, often as part of a major transhumance activity (see page 58).

The high alpine grasslands are wonderful places, and their short growing season makes for a special intensity of colour and life. Gentians, saxifrages, bellflowers, forget-me-nots, louseworts, rock-jasmines, primulas, lilies, orchids and dozens of other plant species vie for the pollination services of the relatively few insects, and we reap the benefit. There are specialist insects, too, such as the Peak White (*Pontia callidice*) and the lovely little Cynthia's Fritillary (*Euphydryas cynthia*), which can be found at heights of over 3,000 m, as well as birds such as the Alpine and Red-billed Choughs (*Pyrrhocorax graculus* and *P. pyrrhocorax*), Water Pipit (*Anthus spinoletta*) and White-winged Snowfinch (*Montifringilla nivalis*).

Once, not so long ago, vast areas of southern France were subject to the grazing pressure of large flocks of sheep, goats and other stock. Such grazing was an integral part of the local economy, and flocks were moved around as necessary to obtain grazing throughout the year, normally accompanied by a shepherd. This occurred most frequently in hilly limestone areas, like the *causses*, the limestone plateaux around Dijon

and many parts of the Dordogne. Although grazing pressure was often intense, it was quite different from the effect of enclosing animals in a field until they eat everything, and many patches would remain as woodland, scrub or long grass, producing a wonderful matrix of near-natural habitats rich in special species. Apart from in a few areas, such as the Pyrenees, La Crau (south-east of Arles) and Haut-Savoie, this practice has declined considerably and huge areas of former grassland are steadily changing. Some are now woodland with few traces of the former grassland, but many exist as rank grass, scrub or light woodland, with an interesting mixture of grassland and woodland species, though each year there is less and less light reaching the ground. In the *causses,* south of Mende and Millau, there are still vast areas of open, species-rich grasslands despite the changes that have taken place.

Heathland

Heathland is more or less the equivalent of old pastures, but on thin, acid soils. Although frequently wild and natural in appearance, it is actually the product of early woodland clearance dating back to the Bronze Age and beyond. Where wood-

land on acid, free-draining soil is cleared and then kept open, the soil tends to develop a particular characteristic profile, known as a podsol, which is very poor in nutrients and may contain a hard layer known as an iron pan. On such soils, the normal replacement vegetation in medium to high rainfall areas is heathland, dominated by relatively few species from the heather family (Ericaceae), such as the Heather (*Calluna vulgaris*) and Bell Heather (*Erica cinerea*). This is not a particularly common habitat in France, and has declined in the last century or so due to agricultural reclamation, afforestation and urban growth. The main areas are on the Cherbourg Peninsula, in hillier parts of Brittany and southwards, in the western Pyrenees and in a few inland areas such as the Sologne. Moorlands such as the Vosges are broadly similar in their vegetation, but are developed over peat in wetter areas, and usually have fewer species.

Although heathland is dominated by just a few species, it is rather good for specialized plants and animals including the

Heath Lobelia (*Lobelia urens*), Smooth Snake (*Coronella austriaca*), Nightjar (*Caprimulgus europaea*), Dartford Warbler (*Sylvia undata*), and a plethora of insects such as tiger beetles (*Cicindela* spp.) and solitary hymenopterans like the fearsome *Bembix rostrata* and Bee Wolf (*Philanthus triangulum*). Heathland is a warm habitat, and often offers the means for species to survive further north than their normal range. It also often occurs in conjunction with active bogs, because it provides a catchment of clear, unpolluted acidic water.

Garrigue

Structurally, *garrigue* is almost the Mediterranean equivalent of heathland, in the sense that it is an open, warm habitat dominated by dwarf shrubs. A low-growing, open community, often with much bare ground, it is usually established on limestone or similar rocks. The main shrubs growing here are *Cistus* spp., Rosemary (*Rosmarinus officinalis*), lavenders (*Lavandula* spp.), Spiny Broom (*Calicotome villosa*), Wild Thyme (*Thymus vulgaris*), sages (*Salvia* spp.) and dwarf forms of many larger shrubs.

The name *garrigue* comes from an old Provencal word, *garriga*, and to many it epitomises the Mediterranean landscape of Provence and elsewhere. *Garrigue* occurs in lovely wild landscapes, often near the sea, and almost all the main plants are aromatic, frequently with strong culinary connections. It is also quite easy to walk across, as it is usually unfenced and there is a high proportion of bare ground. For the naturalist, perhaps its key feature is the wonderful explosion of flowers in late winter and spring (and sometimes again in autumn). Between the shrubs there is a whole community of bulbs and other geophytes, annuals and short-lived herbs that burst into life in the short gap between the winter rains and the intensely hot, dry summers, peaking in April. There are yellow *Fumana* species, pink storksbills (*Erodium* spp.), lovely silvery-leaved, pink-flowered bindweeds (*Convolvulus* spp.), several species of blue, yellow and pink flaxes (*Linum* spp.), and an abundance of orchids including the Man (*Aceras anthropophora*), Bee (*Ophrys apifera*) and Pyramidal (*Anacamptis pyramidalis*) Orchids, tongue orchids (*Serapias* spp.) and many others, some confined to quite limited areas.

Although part of the reason for the open nature of *garrigue* is the hot, dry climate, the grazing and the thin soil, it is also thought that some shrubs use their aromatic oils (mainly terpenes) to effect allelopathy – in other words, to inhibit the growth of their neighbours. The oils may also inhibit insect attack, and possibly cool the surfaces of the plants in hot weather. All plants of *garrigue* are highly adapted to survive the hot, dry summers by disappearing completely back to a seed or bulb, or by specific drought-tolerating adaptations.

Good *garrigue* is also a lovely place to see butterflies such as the Common and Scarce Swallowtails (*Papilio machaon* and *Iphiclides podalirius*), as well as other insects including the European Mantis (*Mantis religiosa*) and the impressive orthopteran *Saga pedo*, and there are usually Stonechats

ABOVE Flower spikes of Heather or Ling, one of the few dominant species on heathland.

BELOW A praying mantis hunting in *garrigue* in late summer.

LAVENDER FIELDS IN PROVENCE

In four Provencal departments – Vaucluse, Drôme, Hautes-Alpes and Alpes de Haute-Provence – summer is characterized by a wonderful explosion of blue stripes as the fields of lavender come into flower. Within these departments, there are at least 40 sq km of lavender fields of all sizes, mostly between the altitudes of 800 and 1,300 m. The main species grown is the Narrow-leaved Lavender (*Lavandula angustifolia*), which is native in the area, but there are also smaller areas of Aspic (*L. latifolia*) and Lavandin (*L. hybrida*). The lavender flowers go mainly for distillation to produce a complex essential oil used in the perfume industry, aromatherapy and various medicinal

products, and even as an insect repellent, and the dried flowers themselves may be used as decoration or in cooking. The industry is significant enough to have sought and received an Appellation d'Origine Contrôlée (AOC) denomination (similar to that used for wines and cheeses) for the best-quality lavender grown in the right area.

By late summer, the Provence countryside is beginning to look a little tired from several months of intense heat and near drought, and there are relatively few flowers about naturally. So, it is not hard to imagine what effect these vast, fragrant, colourful, nectar-rich patches have on the local insect population. Lavender is an attractive plant to insects anyway, but when present in huge quantities in an otherwise rather flowerless landscape, its effect is wonderful. The sound of the honey bees and bumblebees is more of a roar than a hum, as they busily visit every flower.

Often, the lavender fields are close to good habitats such as woodland, scrub and flowery grassland, so the butterflies and other insects pour out of these areas in search of nectar: Scarce and Common Swallowtails, Silver-washed Fritillaries, Dark Green Fritillaries (*Argynnis aglaja*), Painted Ladies (*Vanessa cardui*), Small Tortoiseshells (*Aglais urticae*), several species of white (*Pieris* spp.), and a whole host of blues including less common ones such as the Provence Chalkhill Blue (*Lysandra hispana*). The beautiful blurred shapes of the Hummingbird Hawkmoths (*Macroglossum stellatarum*) are common, bush-crickets such as the Tizi (*Ephippiger ephippiger*) join in, and of course there are predators such as praying mantises (*Stagomantis* spp.) Not bad for a plant used as an insect repellent. Altogether, a visit to a lavender field in summer is a rich experience.

ABOVE A Tizi bush-cricket enjoying the abundance of the lavender fields in late summer.
BELOW A typical late-summer Provence lavender field, surrounded by scrub and woodland.

(*Saxicola torquata*) and wheatears (*Oenanthe* spp.) around, and possibly Short-toed Eagles (*Circaetus gallicus*) hovering overhead. There is good *garrigue* in south-west France, for example around Narbonne, Minerve and Cap Leucate, and in many places in Provence, including on Les Alpilles near Arles. In Corsica, it is uncommon, as most of the rock is granite, but there is some at the southern tip and in a few places elsewhere.

Water and Wetlands

Although not comparable with Scandinavian countries, France is surprisingly well supplied with wetlands and open waters. This is partly due to physical factors such as the many mountain areas and its long coastline, but also to a relatively wet climate and a long history of constructing ponds and lakes for fish rearing, reservoirs and other purposes.

Natural Lakes

The majority of natural lakes are by-products of glaciation. Where ice-sheets or valley glaciers have moved vast quantities of soil and rock around, and deepened parts of valleys below their normal profile, they leave huge amounts of water in their wake when they retreat. Large valley lakes at lower altitudes, such as the Lac du Bourget, north of Chambéry, and Lac d'Annecy in Haute Savoie, are formed in this way, and they are usually large enough and deep enough to have survived as lakes. Generally speaking, lakes tend to gradually fill in over time, unless they are somewhere particularly wet or cold, so many of the smaller or shallower post-glacial valley lakes have

ABOVE A Short-toed Eagle, one of the most distinctive and attractive of the birds that can be seen hunting over open *garrigue*.
BELOW The Lac de Luitel, in the Chaine de Belledonne, is one of the best examples of high-altitude peat bogs and pools.

ABOVE Reed beds and open water in the Domaine de Chérine Reserve near Mezières-en-Brenne.

gone, and may now be interesting bogs or fens, such as the Marais de Lavours in Haute Savoie, or have been converted to agriculture or other uses.

In the higher mountain areas, virtually all the natural lakes are of glacial origin, where a moraine has blocked a valley, or partial deepening by a glacier has left a 'sill' that holds back the water. At this altitude, the climate is usually cool and wet enough for the lakes to remain as open waters, though at more moderate altitudes the shallower ones have often filled in, forming interesting peatland sites such as the attractive Lac Luitel Reserve (now much more bog than *lac*!) at 1,250 m in the Chaine de Belledonne near Grenoble.

There are also a few volcanic crater lakes still remaining in France, particularly in the Auvergne and elsewhere in the Massif Central. These are usually readily distinguishable on maps as they are virtually circular in outline, and of course they only occur in areas that have a recent volcanic history. Mostly, they are similar hydrologically and biologically to lakes of other origins, though their considerable depth in relation to their size and their steep sides can limit their biological diversity. One such lake, Lac Pavin in the Auvergne, is internationally notable in that it is a fine example of a meromictic lake – one in which the lower layers rarely or ever mix with the upper layers. This leads to the lower cold layers being very low in oxygen and inimical to most forms of life except highly specialized ones such as sulphur-using bacteria. For the naturalist, this is a curiosity rather than a special place.

There are a number of large wetland complexes in France, of more or less natural origin, which are of enormous impor-tance to birds and other wildlife. Most are on or near the coast and owe at least part of their origin to the changing sea levels that have taken place since the Ice Age, as marine material has been moved around and terrestrial sites flooded and drained. Major ones include the Grand Brière, the Lac de Grand-Lieu and the Marais Poitevin, all on or near the west coast, and the famous Camargue on the south coast at the mouth of the Rhône River. Whatever their origins, all are marvellous mixtures of open water, marshland or salt marsh, and other wetland habitats, rich in all forms of life.

Manmade Open Waters

The remaining still open waters (that is, excluding rivers) in France are those that are manmade. These vary enormously in their history, purpose and character, but collectively they contribute much to the wildlife importance of France, and a number have international recognition for birds or general wildlife value. In several flat, low-lying parts of the country, there has been a long history of damming streams and rivers to make fish ponds, for example in the Brenne (west of Châteauroux), the Dombes (north-west of Lyon) and the area around Montbrison, north-west of St Etienne, and these have become special places, especially because much of the countryside between the lakes consists of woodland, marshland or unspoiled pasture.

In general, large reservoirs are not of particular interest to the naturalist, especially when they are constructed in steep-

ABOVE The River Ardeche cuts a deep, sinuous gorge through the limestone hills on its way to joining the Rhône north of Avignon.

sided valleys, as their depth and fluctuating water level suits few forms of life. In some situations, however, they can become very valuable for wildlife, especially if they are constructed on relatively flat, low-lying countryside. Two good examples lie to the east of Troyes.

The paired lakes of Lac d'Orient and Lac du Temple lie within an attractive matrix of woodland, marshland and grassland, and are now designated as a Natural Regional Park – La Forêt d'Orient – with nature reserves, hides and plenty of information, as well as an excellent range of birdlife and other species. A little to the north-east, the Lac du Der-Chantecocq is a single vast lake, constructed partly to reduce flooding on the Seine in Paris, and it is now a major ornithological site, noted particularly for its passage and wintering Common Cranes (*Grus grus*), and much else besides (see page 98).

Rivers

In addition to the still waters of France, the rivers must be mentioned, and of course the two overlap as many lakes lie on the courses of rivers, and parts of the larger rivers resemble still waters in the species that occur in them. The longest and probably the most varied of French rivers is the Loire, which rises high in the Massif Central south-east of Le Puy, flowing for 1,012 km and draining almost a fifth of France before empty-

ing into the Atlantic Ocean. Such rivers have an abundance of wildlife, including their own specialities; many fish are confined to rivers, and there are several dragonflies that only breed in rivers and streams, for example the Common Clubtail (*Gomphus vulgatissimus*), Green Snaketail (*Ophiogomphus cecilia*) and Common Goldenring or Golden-ringed Dragonfly (*Cordulegaster boltonii*).

Other Wetland Types

Other wetland habitats (as distinct from open water), usually on a smaller scale, include fens with calcareous groundwater such as those around Berck on the English Channel coast, which are often very rich in flowering plants, and those in the floodplain of smaller calcareous rivers such as the Vézère, which flows into the Dordogne. Bogs are widespread in France, though rarely large. They occur wherever there is acid, nutrient-poor water present for long enough to allow bog mosses (*Sphagnum* spp.) to build up acid peat as they die and decompose. Bogs tend to occur in relatively high rainfall areas on more acid rocks (such as granite or sandstone), often in conjunction with heathland or moorland. It is common for them to gradually encroach on small acidic lakes, forming a surface layer dominated by bog mosses and a few other species. Although bogs are not especially species rich, they do support a number of species that occur almost nowhere else, such as some of the insectivorous plants including sundews (*Drosera* spp.), and dragonflies like the White-faced Darter (*Leucorrhinia dubia*).

DRAGONFLIES AND DAMSELFLIES OF THE BRENNE

In central-western France, lying roughly between the towns of Châteauroux and Châtellerault, there is a fascinating area of low-lying land known as La Brenne, now largely included within the Brenne Natural Regional Park, which covers 1,660 sq km of the Indre department. Collectively, it is regarded as an internationally important wetland, especially for birds, due to the 1,400 or so lakes scattered across its landscape. The lakes are almost entirely of artificial origin, created for fish farming, and many of them are inaccessible or ephemeral, yet taken all together they are also of enormous interest and value for dragonflies and damselflies.

Of course, there are other wetland habitats in addition to the lakes, particularly marshes, streams and rivers, and ample unspoiled terrestrial habitats between the lakes. The exact number of Odonata species is difficult to pinpoint, partly due to incomplete survey data, but also because there is no doubt that some species have invaded while others have declined in recent years. The Natural Park information indicates that two-thirds of French species occur here – that is, 66 species, though it is more likely to be nearer 60 species. In either event, this is a lot of species, and many occur in very large numbers.

This is not the area to see the regional endemics or the specialist upland species, but it is a wonderful place to see a very good range of lowland dragonflies and damselflies. Hawkers such as the Southern Hawker (*Aeshna cyanea*) and Blue Emperor (*Anax imperator*) are common throughout, and you can reasonably expect to see the steadily spreading Lesser Emperor (*A. parthenope*) because the Brenne is well within its present range.

Several skimmer species (*Orthetrum* spp.) are common, and this is also a good place to see the more southerly White-tailed Skimmer (*O. albistylum*) – distinguishable by its white claspers – and the attractive all-blue Southern

ABOVE The lovely Orange-spotted Emerald is one of the rarest dragonfly species to be found in the Brenne.
BELOW A pair of mating Small Red-eyed Damselflies on pondweed – this damselfly species has spread dramatically in recent years.

Skimmer (*O. brunneum*), found principally where there is running water. The Eurasian Basket-tail (*Epitheca bimaculata*), a rather rare and distinctive eastern species, just reaches this far west, where it occurs in deep, well-vegetated and often shaded ponds.

There are several clubtails (*Gomphidae* spp.), including the Common Clubtail (*Gomphus vulgatissimus*) – a species mainly associated with slow-flowing, large rivers – as well as the Yellow Clubtail (*G. simillimus*) and the Western Clubtail (*G. pulchellus*), both essentially south-western species close to the northern edge of their range.

Other dragonfly species that are of interest in this region include the uncommon Orange-spotted Emerald (*Oxygastra curtisii*), which is found along rivers, and several of the white-faced darters such as the Lilypad Whiteface (*Leucorrhinia caudalis*), occurring in the lakes.

Damselflies are abundant and diverse here, including good numbers of the demoiselles (*Calopteryx* spp.), the Common Winter Damsel (*Sympecma fusca*), several species of spreadwing (*Lestes* spp.), four species of bluet (*Coenagrion* spp.), and the two common species of red damselfly, the Large Red Damsel (*Pyrrhosoma nymphula*) and the Small Red Damsel (*Ceriagrion tenellum*). The common and widespread White-legged Damselfly or Blue Featherleg (*Platycnemis pennipes*) is joined by the more southerly Orange Featherleg (*P. acutipennis*), while the attractive Red-eyed Damselfly or Large Redeye (*Erythromma najas*) has recently been joined by the steadily spreading Small Red-eyed Damselfly or Small Redeye (*E. viridulum*). Both species, apart from having distinctive dark blue bodies and red eyes, share the characteristic of using flat, floating leaves such as pondweeds (*Potamogeton* spp.) as their perches.

There are many other good dragonfly areas in France, of course, such as the Camargue and Lorraine Natural Regional Park, but the Brenne is undoubtedly one of the best.

Chapter 2
THE
MOUNTAINS

It is immediately obvious that mountains are special places, something set apart from the world that most of us normally live in, and France is particularly well supplied with such places. Although it does not have quite the same proportion of high land as, say, Switzerland or Austria, it still has a vast area of mountains, in a wonderful variety of forms: the acid-rock rounded Vosges, the limestone peaks and valleys of the Jura, the vast high peaks of the northern Alps, the wonderful warm valleys of the Maritime Alps and the volcanic cones and craters of the Auvergne, to name but a few – all different, and all special.

LEFT The spectacular Gorge de la Jonte cutting its way through the high limestone plateaux of the Massif Central.

FRANCE HAS A VARIETY OF DIFFERENT MOUNTAIN HABITATS, all of which support a wide range of diverse and often strikingly beautiful plant and animal life.

The Mountain Environment

What is it that makes the mountains so different from the point of view of their natural history? The overriding difference is their climate. Gaining altitude is often compared with going northwards (and in fact a direct comparison can be made as far as temperature goes: moving up 100 m on a mountain is roughly equivalent to moving 80 km towards the pole). As air from the lowlands rises, it expands and cools at an approximate rate of 1° per 100 m gain in altitude – a very significant rate of temperature loss. At the same time, it becomes increasingly likely as the air rises that it will shed its humidity as rain or other precipitation. So, as a general rule, the higher you go in mountains, the colder and wetter it becomes, though there are many exceptions.

If you can go high enough, eventually mountains become drier, as all the rain has been shed leaving dry air, but this is scarcely relevant in France. However, there are many rain-shadow areas within and around the mountains, where the prevailing damp winds are interrupted by a mountain range and forced to shed their humidity, so that anything to the lee side is much drier than anything on the windward side. The west side of the Vosges, for example, is much wetter than the east side in the Rhône Valley; Briançon, perched between the northern and southern French Alps at 1,300 m, has 300 days of sunshine a year, more than Nice, and low rainfall, due to being in a rain shadow from almost every direction. Yet only 15 km away, at Le Monêtier les Bains, the rainfall is well over three times as great, and temperatures are much lower. Although you can generalize about the alpine climate, you can be certain that there will be many variations and exceptions, and they are not always easy to predict.

As well as the effects of altitude, in a large country like France the effects of latitude are very significant, too. The mountains of Corsica and the Maritime Alps are much warmer at a given altitude than the Vosges and Jura, for example, and this is reflected in the natural tree-line height, which varies between 1,200 and 1,300 m in the Vosges, through 1,800 and

OPPOSITE The magnificent 'Grand Canyon of Verdon' cuts its way through dramatic and rarely visited mountains rising to 2,000 m.
BELOW A particularly dramatic part of the French Alps, known as the Casse Déserte, on the Col d'Izoard in winter.

BELOW High forests and peaks around the Spelunca Valley in the mountains of Corsica.

2,000 m in the northern Alps, and up to 2,400 m in the southern Alps and the Pyrenees. Broad climatic patterns have their effect, too, and the more westerly mountains exposed to the effects of the Atlantic, such as the western Pyrenees and the Auvergne, have a different climate from mountains of a similar height and latitude further east. The Massif Central is particularly interesting, as it is possible to determine three climatic types within it – oceanic (Atlantic), continental and Mediterranean, depending on the part of the *massif* you are in.

In any case, one thing is clear – the mountain climate is almost invariably harsher than the climate of the surrounding lowlands. Unlike in polar areas, where the whole region is subject to the same climate, the areas of alpine climate can lie geographically close to areas with a quite different lowland climate. Alpine regions differ from polar ones in other ways, too, particularly in the day-length pattern, which does not have the extremes of daylight length experienced by the poles. In the

alpine summer the days may not be especially long, but the level of insolation is much higher, which can be a problem or an opportunity, depending on the situation and on the species concerned. Further south, even at high altitude, there will also be warm days in the winter period when activity may be possible, which is not the case at the poles in winter.

The higher you go, the greater the likelihood there is of snow, and the longer the snow is likely to lie. This has an enormous effect on the alpine species, and also on the surrounding areas, as the snow accumulation in the mountains acts as a vast reservoir for the rivers, releasing water slowly throughout the summer. At very high elevations, snow can fall in almost any month, and certainly falls regularly in at least six months of the year except in the warmest or driest of mountain areas.

The colder it is, the more snow accumulates, and finally a point is reached where it rarely melts at all – the snowline. Not surprisingly, this is not a clear-cut line as such. Apart from the enormous variation between years, and the steady climatic drift like the one we are experiencing at the moment, there are many variations even within one area. North-facing slopes are

much colder than south-facing ones, so snow melts more slowly on them, though this may be balanced by more snow coming in on winds from the south. Steeper areas, especially if they are at more than 60°, rarely hold much snow, and particularly windy places, such as cols, may lose their snow early. In the Alps, the level of the permanent snowline varies between about 2,400 m and 3,000 m, though this is changing as the effects of global warming begin to bite. In places where snow never melts, glaciers begin to form as the pressure of snow and ice building up eventually squeezes out a tongue of ice, which flows down a valley that is at least partly of its own making.

There are rather few glaciers in the French Alps, for various reasons, and those that do exist are retreating. The best are in the Massif des Ecrins, such as the Glacier Blanc on the Barre des Ecrins, or La Meije, so spectacularly visible from the village of La Grave in the Romanche Valley; or the famous glaciers on the north side of Mont Blanc near Chamonix, including the best known of all, the Mer de Glace.

This glacier rises at 3,900 m on the slopes of Mont Blanc and descends to 1,400 m over a length of 5.6 km, almost to

ABOVE A wonderful natural rock garden on limestone in the Maritime Alps below the Col de Restefond.

within sight of Chamonix (in fact, it used to be in sight of Chamonix, but has retreated in recent years in common with most other glaciers, moving, in places, at up to 120 m per year). From the wildlife point of view, glaciers are not of special direct relevance now, as they cover such a small area, but their cumulative effect on the mountain landscape through colder periods has been vast. Despite the harshness of the mountain climate, many plants and animals live under these conditions, and many have evolved to such an extent that they can no longer live anywhere else.

Plants

As you climb up through a mountainous area, from about 1,500 m upwards (varying according to the latitude) the trees begin to thin out and become more stunted. Trees are unable to grow under conditions that are too harsh, especially where there is heavy snow and thin soil, and this starts to become

ABOVE The Arolla Pine is one of the hardiest of alpine trees, surviving severe winter cold and deep snow.

ABOVE The beautiful cushions of Moss Campion (*Silene acaulis*) are covered with pink flowers in early summer.

noticeable as the zone known as the natural tree-line is approached. Some species, such as the Arolla Pine (*Pinus cembra*), are clearly better adapted to surviving at higher altitudes, and it is generally true that most of the higher-altitude trees are evergreen. At first sight this seems counter-intuitive, as the leaves are exposed to the long rigours of winter, but it appears that the advantages of not having to find the resources to produce new – and often vulnerable – leaves each spring outweigh any problems of surviving through the winter.

At the very highest levels of tree growth in the Alps, there is a real mountain specialist, the Dwarf Pine, which never fully grows into a tree and instead forms dense scrub woodland, 2–5 m in height, often known as *krummholz*. Such trees or bushes are not only dwarf, but also often heavily deformed, with little growth on the windward side and strong growth away from the wind. These high-altitude trees may be very old, as their growth is slow and the effects of fungal and insect attack are very limited here. The oldest trees in the world, the Bristlecone Pines (*Pinus longaeva*) of California, grow at altitudes of up to almost 4,000 m, and the oldest specimens are nearly 5,000 years old.

Above this slightly nebulous and certainly variable tree-line, there is a huge area of more open land consisting of grass-land, dwarf shrubs such as Bilberry (*Vaccinium myrtillus*), Trailing Azalea (*Loiseleuria procumbens*) and Arctic Bearberry (*Arctostaphylos alpina*), and ultimately scree, rock and bare ground. As already mentioned, the natural tree-line has almost invariably been lowered in French mountains by the long-standing activity of humans and their grazing animals, so this

open alpine zone, above the trees, is much more extensive than it would otherwise be. In Savoie, for example, these high *alpages* cover 1,650 sq km, or about a quarter of the area of the department.

This huge, wonderful and largely unspoiled high alpine area is the place for the real alpine specialists, many of which are confined to such areas and highly adapted to them. In order to deal with the severe problems of extreme cold, periodic heat, short growing season, high winds, thin soil and frequently high summer rainfall, plants have to adapt. Many alpine plants share characteristics such as a very dwarfed growth habit (it is warmer and less windy near the ground), long-lived, leathery and hairy leaves that take less effort to constantly replace, and a very high ratio of root growth to above-ground parts. They are also well adapted to prevent water loss. At the higher levels virtually all plants are long-lived perennials, as it is too risky a strategy to reproduce each year, and grow from seed to flower in a short, unreliable growing season. There are a few annuals, such as the pretty Snow Gentian (*Gentiana nivalis*), which somehow survive at heights of up to 3,000 m, but these are oddities.

At the highest levels, even the small flowering plants begin to peter out, though some really hardy specialists go remarkably high. Some small saxifrages such as the Scree Saxifrage (*Saxifraga androsacea*) and Purple Saxifrage (*S. oppositifolia*) reach as high as 3,800 m, the beautiful little pink Alpine Rock Jasmine (*Androsace alpina*) goes as high as 4,000 m, while the extraordinary Glacier Crowfoot (*Ranunculus glacialis*) reaches an exceptional 4,250 m elsewhere in the Alps. Some lichens

ABOVE One of the most widespread of the subshrubs that grow above the tree-line is the tiny Trailing Azalea, usually found on acid soils.

ABOVE The Spring Gentian is an iconic high alpine flower due to its vivid bright blue colour.

and bryophytes become more common at high altitudes. The attractive lichen *Solorina crocea* does particularly well around high snow patches, Map Lichen (*Rhizocarpon geographicum*) seems to go as high as there are rocks for it to grow on, while bryophytes such as *Lophocolea sudetica* and *Anthelia juratzkana* both grow at very high altitudes. In general, it seems that the biggest factor in inhibiting plant growth is usually the lack of soil, rather than the climate itself.

One of the wonderful side effects of life at high altitudes is that the flowers are often strikingly beautiful. There is no simple reason for this, but it relates mainly to the relative shortage of insect pollinators at high altitudes. It is harder for insects to adapt to harsh climates, so there are fewer around relative to the number of flowers. In order to attract pollinators, therefore, the flowering plants have evolved strategies such as having very bright, attractive flowers, producing dense clumps of flowers visible from further away, such as the rock jasmines (*Androsace* spp.) and Moss Campion (*Silene acaulis*), or producing plenty of nectar and a strong scent. All of these are features that we can appreciate, despite the fact that they are not intended for us! Some plants, such as the Alpine Bistort (*Polygonum viviparum*), hedge their bets by producing normal fertile flowers in part of the spike, and bulbils in the remainder. These latter can simply drop off and grow without any fertilization required, and they are large enough to give the new plant a good start in its short growing season.

In general, the diversity of cold high-altitude areas is inherently lower than that of equivalent warmer areas. They *seem* particularly rich and diverse for several reasons. As noted above, the flowers are particularly intense and grow in great abundance, producing a wonderful effect; this is strengthened by the relatively short flowering season, which cannot begin in earnest until the snow melts. In the higher mountains a very high proportion of natural and semi-natural habitats remains – and these are the most flowery places – whereas in most lowland areas, virtually all of the former flowery open habitats have been replaced by intensive agriculture or have degraded to some degree, so that the relicts are not a true representation of the potential biodiversity.

Butterflies

The mountain ranges of France, and especially the most southerly ranges, support the greatest diversity of butterfly species. In the Pyrenees and Maritime Alps, for example, it is not unreasonable to expect to see 100 or more species in a week-long visit in July. Part of the reason for this abundance and diversity is the simple fact that there is far more unspoiled natural or semi-natural habitat available in mountains than in most lowland areas and, crucially, it is all joined up into one vast interconnected resource. But there are also mountain specialists, butterflies that only occur in the mountains and differ to a greater or lesser degree from their lowland relatives. Many widespread species have mountain forms or subspecies, which are often both smaller and darker than their lowland equivalents, and there are also quite distinct mountain species.

The lower areas of mountains are clearly optimal habitats – warm, flowery and unspoiled – but the high areas pose quite a different set of problems. The growing and flying seasons are

very short (and conversely the resting season as egg, larva or pupa is very long), particularly in years following heavy winter snow. Also, many days within this short season will be cold, wet, foggy or even snowy, and it will regularly be very windy. Clearly the high-altitude specialists have to be hardy and well adapted, though curiously there is no obvious set of characters that they have all adopted. The Apollo (*Parnassius apollo*) is very large and almost white (though admittedly it is not a real high-altitude specialist, usually occurring below 2,000 m), whereas the Sooty Ringlet (*Erebia pluto*) is small and dark, and all other combinations exist. There is a slight tendency for mountain species to be darker and/or smaller than their lowland equivalents, but this certainly does not apply generally.

There are at least 20 butterfly species in France that can be reasonably described as high-altitude specialists. The group with the most such species is the ringlets (*Erebia* spp.) in the family Satyridae, most of which are mountain butterflies up to at least mid-altitude range, with the Sooty Ringlet (*Erebia pluto*) and Silky Ringlet (*E. gorge*) going particularly high. There are several whites, notably the Mountain Small White (*Pieris ergenae*) and the remarkable Peak White (*Pontia callidice*) – the latter is found at well over 3,000 m and seems to be able to fly in almost any weather. Two clouded yellows specialize in higher mountain areas – the Moorland Clouded Yellow (*Colias palaeno*) in more acid areas and the Mountain Clouded Yellow (*C. phicomone*) elsewhere.

The Alpine Grayling (*Oeneis glacialis*) is a specialist of high, rocky slopes and screes around the tree-line, and the Alpine Heath (*Coenonympha gardetta*) occurs in high, grassy areas at up to about 2,500 m. The blues are abundant at mid-altitudes, though only a few regularly live higher up, noticeably the Glandon Blue (*Agriades glandon*) and Gavarnie Blue (*A. pyrenaicus*), which are closely related and rather small and dull, and the Alpine Blue (*Albulina orbitulus*), a lovely, intensely blue butterfly that only occurs above about 1,500 m. Among the fritillaries, there are many that revel in the mid-altitude grasslands, though a few, such as Titania's Fritillary (*Clossiana titania*) and particularly the gorgeous little Cynthia's Fritillary (*Hypodryas cynthia*) – a real mountain specialist that occurs at heights of up to and beyond 3,000 m – occur at higher levels.

Birds and Mammals

These have a rather different relationship with high altitudes than plants, as most of them are able to move readily to lower, warmer situations if required, whereas plants and, to a considerable degree, insects, have to stay at high altitude throughout

TOP, LEFT The Apollo butterfly is a distinctive mountain species, commonly found at altitudes of up to 2,000 m.
CENTRE, LEFT Grison's Fritillary (*Mellicta varia*) occurs on flowery mountain slopes at up to about 2,500 m in the Alps.
BOTTOM, LEFT The Mountain Ringlet (*Erebia epiphron*), one of the many ringlets to be found in mountain areas.

the winter. For example, large numbers of birds migrate into mountain areas to breed through the period when conditions are remarkably good, then leave as soon as the weather deteriorates. Mammals are rather less mobile, but many have a cycle of vertical migration, moving up the mountains to find food and escape parasites in summer, then coming down again in winter. There are also a number of birds and animals that are not particularly adapted to mountain life, but are nowadays confined to it because they have been ousted from the rest of the intensively used countryside, such as the Brown Bear (*Ursus arctos*), Eurasian Lynx (*Lynx lynx*), Wildcat (*Felis silvestris*) and Golden Eagle (*Aquila chrysaetos*).

A few birds breed in the mountains and remain there for the whole year, and are clearly well adapted to the mountain environment. The Ptarmigan (*Lagopus mutus*) is a supreme example, remaining high in the mountains all year (though it moves around as necessary within its area) and changing its plumage up to four times a year to try to remain camouflaged in all seasons to escape notice from its main predator, the Golden Eagle. The Alpine Accentor (*Prunella collaris*), the lovely little White-winged Snowfinch (*Montifringilla nivalis*), the Alpine Chough (*Pyrrhocorax graculus*) and the fabulous Wallcreeper (*Tichodroma muraria*) are all year-round mountain birds that are more or less confined to mountains, though all of them practise a certain amount of vertical migration, coming down to warmer, more food-rich sites in winter.

ABOVE The strikingly beautiful Eurasian Lynx is gradually recolonizing French mountains after becoming extinct in many areas.
BELOW The Alpine Chough is one of a small group of hardy bird species that spend most of their lives at high altitude in the mountains.

Among the mammals of the high mountain areas, the Snow Vole (*Microtus nivalis*) has the most extreme life history. Snow Voles occur at altitudes of over 4,000 m on the slopes of Mont Blanc, though more commonly they are found at heights of between 2,000 and 3,000 m. They burrow under the soil, but

ABOVE One of the many important peatland areas on the wetter western slopes of the Vosges Mountains.

continue to remain active right through the winter, with their winter burrows wandering freely between snow and soil. When the snow melts in spring, their loose colonies are often very visible, because so many of their burrows reach the now snow-free surface of the ground. Interestingly, some studies have shown that they are very social in summer, but rather solitary in winter, perhaps because food is in shorter supply.

Reptiles and Amphibians

A surprising number of species of herpetofauna (reptiles and amphibians) are resident in high mountain areas, though none can be said to be mountain specialists, except perhaps Orsini's Viper (*Vipera ursinii*), which rarely occurs below 1,000 m and appears at up to 2,500 m or more. The species occurring at the highest altitudes are Lanza's Alpine Salamander (*Salamandra lanzai*), found at up to 2,300 m in the Maritime Alps; the Palmate Newt (*Triturus helveticus*), up to 2,500 m in the Pyrenees; Alpine Newt (*T. alpestris*), up to 2,650 m in the Alps; Common Frog (*Rana temporaria*), up to 2,800 m in the Alps; and Wall Lizard (*Podarcis muralis*), up to 2,200 m, all impressive figures for cold-blooded animals with little mobility.

The Mountain Regions

The whole eastern side of France, where it adjoins Germany, Switzerland and Italy, consists almost entirely of mountains. The most northerly part is made up of the Vosges, which lie entirely in France, though they share many similarities with the Palatinate Forest (or Pfälzerwald) to the north, and the Black Forest (or Schwarzwald) to the east. The Northern Vosges and the Palatinate Forest collectively make up a huge UNESCO Biosphere Reserve: Palatinate-Forest–Vosges du Nord, covering over 3,000 sq km, though most of this is poorly protected 'transition zone'.

The Vosges are ancient, rounded mountains, made up of hard sandstones and crystalline, often acidic rocks, including granite, reaching to 1,424 m at their highest point. Despite their relative lack of height, they form a major climatic, ecological and social barrier, so that the character of the rather dry Rhine Valley to the east is quite different from that of the undulating, well-watered Lorraine country to the west. The Vosges are the coolest of France's mountains. They have much more in common with the more northerly German or even Scandinavian mountains, and several northerly species find their most southerly outposts in Europe here, such as the Bog Arum (*Calla palustris*).

The Vosges are well wooded partly because the climate and soil do not suit many other uses, with forests dominated by Norway Spruce, Silver Fir, Common Beech, oaks and pines. The highest summits are open grassland or moorland, known locally as *ballons*. On the west side, there are a number of important bogs and small lakes, such as the Tourbière de Machais, while on the east side there are more grasslands, including some lovely limestone grasslands rich in flowers around the village of Bollenberg.

The Jura Mountains commence immediately to the south of the Vosges, roughly from Besançon or Montbéliard southwards, straddling the French–Swiss border for most of its length. Although only slightly higher than the Vosges (reaching 1,718 m at their highest point, the Crêt de la Neige), the Jura Mountains are quite different in character. The biggest difference is that they are largely made up of hard limestone (the origin of the word 'jurassic'), with a much more angular and spectacular scenery, and a greater warmth and lightness.

The series of folds making up the Jura Mountains is of relatively recent origin, geologically speaking, and it still defines the surface landscape. The underlying rock not only affects the scenery, but also leads to differences in land use. The more freely draining soils, along with the warmer climate, have led to a relatively high degree of pastoralism here historically, and

ABOVE Wetlands and pastureland in the Drugeon Valley, a particularly species-rich area of the Jura Mountains.

some arable farming, while the Vosges are largely forested, with both natural and plantation woodlands. The Vosges form a fairly narrow, humpbacked range, with rivers running both directly and rapidly out to east or west, whereas the Jura Mountains are much more convoluted and broader, with many rivers running in longitudinal valleys, roughly northwards or southwards, often slowing down and forming lakes in the flatter high-altitude Jura valleys. This gives the Jura a considerably more varied character and a wider range of habitats, and the underlying limestone soil has given rise to a richer flora.

The southern part of the Jura, roughly from Morez southwards, is known as the Haut Jura, and it has a higher and wilder character than the lower, more northerly parts. Eastwards, the Jura Mountains extend into Switzerland, and northwards they continue, though at lower elevations, into Germany in a north-east trending arc.

The climate of the Jura is notably continental, with warm, dry summers and cold winters, and some of the intermontane plateaux and valleys experience perhaps the coldest winters of any inhabited areas in France, with a record -41°C noted on one occasion.

ABOVE The Col de Larche and mountains along the Italian border in the Mercantour National Park, seen here in early winter while the larches are still a fiery orange colour.

Almost seamlessly, the Alps begin to the south of the Jura, and run from there in an uninterrupted swathe down to the Mediterranean at Nice and the Italian border. Although this region only occupies a tiny part of France's surface area, its value is inestimable, and it seems vastly larger when you are in it due to the convoluted terrain and high peaks within it. It is a wonderful area for the naturalist, and the habitats are much more varied than you might expect. It is so large and so geologically and climatically varied that almost all habitats are found here, often in vast areas. The total number of species is hard to estimate, but it is huge, and a very high proportion of France's plants and animals occur within the region.

The northern section, around Chamonix and along the border with Switzerland and north-west Italy, contains the highest peaks and the longest glaciers, including the highest mountain in Europe (as long as you do not consider the Caucasus to be part of Europe!), the granite peak of Mont Blanc, at 4,808 m. There are a number of different figures for the height of Mont Blanc – this may be partly because it is still rising, but more likely because the highest point lies on ice that varies in thickness; the highest rock point is actually just below 4,800 m.

Southwards from here there is a vast area of high mountains, beginning with the great Massif de la Vanoise – all included in the Vanoise National Park, the first in France – reaching a maximum height of 3,855 m. This park is large – it has a peripheral zone of 1,480 sq km and a core zone of 530 sq km, made effectively larger by adjoining the marvellous Gran Paradiso National Park in Italy. Vanoise lies in Savoie, and Chamonix lies in Haute-Savoie, and these two departments epitomize the French Alps, with most of the high peaks, much of the transhumance (see page 58), and a wonderful range of flora, fauna and scenery.

Continuing the journey southwards, there are more fine areas. South-west of Vanoise, or due west of Briançon, lies the fabulous Massif des Ecrins, all within the National Park des Ecrins, which covers almost 2,700 sq km in its core and peripheral areas. This is an astonishing area of high, inaccessible peaks drained by valleys running out in all directions, with a wonderful variety of habitats and landscapes, and an exceptionally rich flora and fauna. Within the park boundaries there is an altitude range of 800–4,102 m, 170 sq km of glaciers, 367.5 sq km of high summer grazing pastures (*alpages*) and more than 30 sq km of forests, together with many lesser habitats such as lakes, fens and cliffs. There are also at least 1,800 species of higher plant and about 65 species of mammal, to name but a couple of groups.

Much less known is the Queyras area to the south-east of Briançon, in a large, enclosed valley running up to the Italian border. This is a much quieter area, with peaks reaching up to well over 3,000 m all around, and a notably rich flora of more

than 2,000 species. It also includes the highest village in France, St Veran, at almost exactly 2,000 m altitude.

A little further south, beyond Barcelonette and the Ubaye Valley, lie the Maritime Alps. Though not generally as high as the more northerly Alps, reaching to just over 3,000 m, the Maritime Alps are a wonderfully special area, with a warm, sunny climate, lovely scenery and far fewer visitors than the high Alps.

Part of the area is covered by the Mercantour National Park – a superbly species-rich area with more than 2,000 species of flower (of which 40 are endemic and 220 are considered very rare), as well as 53 endangered vertebrates. In effect, the Alps continue on into Corsica, a surprisingly mountainous island with peaks as high as Mont Cinto (2,706 m) rising from a wonderful unspoiled, wooded Mediterranean landscape.

Westwards from the Alps there is a further area of rather amorphous mountain ranges, not as high as the Alps, but collectively forming a magnificent block of largely unspoiled land. Much of inland Provence is mountainous, with well-known peaks such as Mont Ventoux (1,909 m) and Montagne Ste Victoire (1,011 m), but also many lesser-known and barely visited ranges, such as the limestone peaks north of the great Gorge du Verdon, reaching up to 2,000 m. A little further north there are some lovely pre-alpine ranges including the beautiful Chaine de Belledonne, just north-east of Grenoble, which has much of the character of the Alps, but few of the visitors; and the delightful Massif des Bauges between Annecy and Chambery, now largely included in a Natural Regional Park.

My personal favourite of these mountains squeezed between the Rhône Valley and the high Alps is the Vercors, an extraordinarily spectacular range of limestone mountains, whose eastern cliffs seem to hang over Grenoble and the area south of there. Due to their alignment and relatively recent folding, they reach the surface as a dramatic collection of cliffs and peaks on the east side, with beautiful forests and pastures flowing around them. Above the cliffs there is a high plateau and a complex series of gorges. For the naturalist, they are extraordinary, with a fantastic combination of alpine, Mediterranean and northern species, particularly rich in orchids. North of Grenoble, the same formation continues, though slightly lower, as the beautiful and largely wooded Massif de la Chartreuse.

The Rhône River, on its way southwards from the Swiss Alps to the Mediterranean, cuts a deep valley through this part of France, known in French as the *sillon rhodanien* (literally 'the furrow of the Rhône'). To the west of it lies the great group of mountains and hills known collectively as the Massif Central, filling much of the land between Lyon and Limoges. This is a highly complicated area, with particularly convoluted geological formations that are largely associated with volcanic and plutonic activity.

Southwards from Clermont-Ferrand lies a vast area of volcanic rock, the Cantal volcanism, which covers 2,700 sq km (the largest such area in Europe), reaching to 1,886 m at its highest point, and known collectively as the Auvergne. It is a wonderful area, not only for the marvellous examples of all facets of volcanism, but also for its long history of habitation, beautiful scenery and rich flora and fauna. Much of the agriculture remains traditional, and there are large areas of flowery pastures and woodland, and miles of hedges with trees. There is another area of volcanic rock around Le Puy-en-Velay, famous for its buildings on volcanic 'plugs', and the source of the Loire.

RIGHT A spectacular view in the lovely Vercors Mountains, looking across a hay meadow to the distinctive peak of Mont Aiguilles soon after dawn.

ABOVE An old volcano in the Auvergne – a marvellous region in the Massif Central containing many species of animal and plant.

Much of the rest of this area is underlain by granite, which tends to form acidic, water-retaining soil that usually remains well wooded. The Cévennes, including the National Park, lies partly on the granite. Its highest peak is at Mont Lozère (1,699 m), and there are other peaks such as Mont Aigoual (1,565 m) on granite and gneiss. The southern parts of the region are principally made up of Jurassic limestone, giving rise to a distinctive scenery of hills, plateaux, cliffs and gorges. In the east, around Millau, it forms high plateaux at about 1,000 m – known as the *causses* – still largely covered by ancient flowery grassland, and dissected into deep, spectacular gorges such as the Gorges du Tarn and Gorge de la Jonte. Further west, towards the Dordogne, the hills are lower and more cultivated. The whole area has a wonderfully warm, rich feeling about it, with a very long history of human habitation, and a superb flora and fauna.

And so to the Pyrenees, the most isolated and, in some ways, the most dramatic of France's mountains. They rise so suddenly from the plains of south-west France, and occupy the 430-km neck of the peninsula separating France from Spain so completely, that their visual, social, climatic and ecological effect is quite astonishing. On the French side, to the north, they fall quite rapidly to the lowlands, in contrast to the more convoluted series of lower ranges to be found on the Spanish side, and there are many places in this part of France from where a vast panorama of the Pyrenees can be seen. Geologically they are complex, though largely made up of plutonic and sedimentary rocks rather than volcanic rocks. There are large areas of granite, gneiss, sandstone and schist, with smaller pockets of limestone, mainly confined to lower areas. On the north side, in particular, there are some superbly dramatic cirques, where small ice sheets have formed on the north faces and gouged

their way out – the best examples are in the central Pyrenees, including the famous cirques at Gavarnie and Troumouse. The highest peak is the Pic d'Aneto (3,404 m), which is just in Spain, but there are many French peaks of over 3,000 m. Because of the Pyrenees' isolated position, warm climate and access to animal life in both France and the Iberian Peninsula, its flora and fauna are notably rich, with many endemic species found nowhere else. For example, the flora of the Pyrenees (including the Spanish side) amounts to about 4,500 species, of which 160 are endemic to some degree. There are also over 200 species of butterfly, some special cave insects and many endemic vertebrates such as the Pyrenean Desman (*Galemys pyrenaicus*) (see Chapter 6) and three species of rock-lizard (see Chapter 7), all in wonderful, largely unspoiled mountain scenery.

Transhumance

Transhumance is seasonal mass movement of stock (cattle, sheep or horses) and humans from one area to another. It can include various relatively small-scale movements, but as far as we are concerned here, of most significance is the major movement of animals from the southern lowlands of France (especially Provence) into the mountains for the summer. This process happens because the Mediterranean lands can support relatively few animals through the hot, dry summers, whereas the high pastures of the mountains are at their productive and nutritious best in high summer. It is akin to the mass migration of antelopes and deer elsewhere in the world, but differs here in that it is directed entirely by humans.

Transhumance is a very ancient practice (at least in some areas), which goes back to prehistoric times, though the widespread movements from Provence to the Alps are more recent. It has always waxed and waned, affected by the price of wool and meat, the climate, wars and so on, but currently it is reasonably stable. In 1802, a new breed of hybrid sheep, the Mérino d'Arles, was produced, and it proved to be the ideal transhumance animal – hardy, productive and with strong gregarious instincts – giving a boost to the process, and starting a trend towards sheep rather than cattle.

Nowadays, transhumance in France is a curious and appealing combination of traditional and sophisticated. There is more machinery and vehicular transport, and there are collective organizations with websites and political muscle, exclusive appelations (AOC) for special mountain cheeses and a range of specially bred stock varieties; yet at the other extreme it may involve whole families moving from home for months, often walking for hundreds of miles, and contributing to a rich and varied semi-natural environment. This is undoubtedly a low-input–low-output economy, and the areas that the animals graze in summer are rarely fertilized or managed in any way other than by grazing. Today, there is state aid for the process in various ways, including 100 per cent payments for animals lost to the few Grey Wolves (*Canis lupus*) that have been creeping back into the French alpine area since 1992.

Much the largest movement takes place from the Provence area into the southern and central Alps, involving at least 1.6 million sheep, about 500,000 cows, more than 5,000 goats and about 20,000 horses. This is a considerable amount of grazing power, and while occasionally one may regret that an area has been overgrazed, in general the grazing plays an important role in maintaining the flora and fauna of the alpine and subalpine parts of the Alps. There is also a degree of transhumance up into the southern parts of the Massif Central, mainly on the limestone, and into the Pyrenees, though both have declined in recent decades. Today there are not enough animals to maintain the limestone *causses* as grass-

ABOVE A Provencal family and its huge flock of sheep passing through the Maritime Alps on its way north to higher pastures.
BELOW Cattle grazing in the high montane pastures of the Volcans d'Auvergne Regional Natural Park.

land, and some are steadily drifting to scrub or woodland. In the Pyrenees, cattle are the most important animals, and there are many special local cheeses.

Chapter 3
COASTAL FRANCE

The coast of France is long, varied and fascinating. Depending on how you measure it, the total length is roughly 5,500 km including Corsica, though the convoluted coast of Brittany is notoriously difficult to measure and some estimates add another 1,000 km to this length. Official estimates, based on the total of 5,500 km, show that it is made up of about 1,948 km of sandy coasts, 1,316 km of salt marshes and mudflats, and 2,269 km of rocky coasts including cliffs, though of course these simple figures mask an additional wonderful variety of geology, aspect, colour, vegetation and wilderness.

LEFT Headland on the Crozon Peninsula in Brittany, one of France's most rugged regions.

The Atlantic is a huge major ocean with almost continuous strong swells from the west, a typical salinity of about 35 parts per thousand, and a very significant tidal range, with a marked difference between high and low tide. This varies, but it is about 6–8 m in Brittany on average. By contrast, the Mediterranean, though by no means always calm, has no steady, relentless swell, is rather more saline (about 38 parts per thousand) and has an extremely small tidal range of no more than 5–10 cm, depending on where you are and the state of the moon. These differences may not sound like much, but they collectively have a consider-

T HE COAST OF FRANCE DIVIDES NEATLY INTO TWO quite different zones: the Atlantic coast and the Mediterranean coast (the North Sea coast is essentially an inlet of the Atlantic, though some of the effects of the Atlantic diminish progressively as you move eastwards). They lie in completely different and distinctive climatic zones, and are named the Atlantic and Mediterranean climatic zones after the names of the seas that define them. They are also different in other ways, because the two seas are so different.

ABOVE The granite coast of north Brittany at Ile Grande, full of rockpools and secret inlets.
BELOW Flowery sand dunes – many protected by nature reserve status – stretch along the sheltered eastern coasts of the Quiberon Peninsula.

able effect on the shape of the coast and on what lives there, especially when combined with the different climates.

The exposed west-facing Atlantic coasts of France have a very distinctive character. Sandy areas are dominated by dunes made up from sand blown inland by the steady westerly winds, and wherever hard rock reaches the surface, there are exposed rocky cliffs and headlands. It is only in sheltered inlets or in the lees of peninsulas that salt marshes and mudflats can develop, because here the silt is not constantly washed away. Where rivers meet the sea, they form estuaries that are almost completely emptied and refilled with sea water twice a day, thus producing a distinctive but harsh environment where fresh water meets salt water. In the Mediterranean these erosion processes are much less marked, and long stretches of coast (for instance between Perpignan and Marseille) are dominated by lagoons, salt marshes and intervening beaches, which simply would not survive under exposed Atlantic conditions. The additional salinity, which is not vastly different, but is steadily increasing in the Mediterranean due to the effects of the Suez Canal, the damming of the Nile and other factors, has some effect on the animals and plants that can survive in it. There is quite a noticeable difference between the flora and fauna of the Mediterranean and the Atlantic, due partly to this difference in salinity.

Because of the much lower tidal range in the Mediterranean, the mouths of rivers form completely

different structures compared with those on the Atlantic coast. When the river reaches the sea it soon drops its load of heavier sediment, which then builds up into an area of low-lying habitat at the margins of sea and land. River channels constantly change course as they become blocked by silt, vegetation and other material, areas flood then drain, and gradually a vast area of new land builds up. Within it, there are lagoons, severed portions of old river courses, wet woodland, salt marsh and other habitats.

Often, the material that is carried out to sea is washed up and blown back inland to form sand dunes at the outer margins. The whole area is usually called a delta, quite different in form to an estuary, with different habitats and different inhabitants. There are many deltas in the Mediterranean, but really only one of significance in France, at the mouth of the Rhône, and the associated mouth of the Durance – the Camargue and

the Crau. This is a superb example of a delta, with many of the classical habits of such a site, though admittedly not quite in their natural state.

The Coastal Environment

The plants and animals that live on and around the coast are often very different from those that live inland. There are many species, from all groups, which are confined to the coast, and others that are much more common towards the coast. Why should this be so?

The climate is a major contributing factor. Coastal areas tend to be more moderate climatically than inland areas, milder in winter and cooler in summer. This is most marked on the Atlantic coast, where the huge bulk of the ocean combined with frequent winds from the west tends to even up the temperature difference between land and sea. As it happens, the Atlantic coasts are generally wetter than inland areas, though this does not always apply to coastal areas. Because there is a

ABOVE The attractive Kerry Lily becomes increasingly confined to coastal parts of France in the north because it is sensitive to heavy frosts.
BELOW The Penerf Estuary in Brittany, part of the vast extent of intertidal lands to be found around the Atlantic coasts of France.

denticulate) and Kerry Lily (Simethis planifolia) – that live on the coast because they cannot tolerate either long, dry periods in summer, or long, colder periods in winter. Typically, this is more noticeable in plants, and among animals is most often seen in invertebrates, as they are less able to make seasonal migrations. Frequently, such species become more and more confined to the coast towards the north, indicating that cold winters are the most significant limiting factor.

Coastal areas additionally tend to be more windy than inland areas, especially but not exclusively on the Atlantic coasts. This restricts the stature of plants, limits insects' ability to fly, reduces tree growth, moves more soil around and tends to produce more areas of bare ground. Certain plants clearly thrive under these conditions, and sometimes it is clear that it is the openness they like rather than the mildness, because they often also occur in the other great open habitat of France – high mountain areas. Good examples of such plants include Thrift (*Armeria maritima*), Common Scurvy-Grass (*Cochlearia officinalis*), Roseroot (*Sedum rosea*) and many lichens.

strong tendency for weather to arrive from the Atlantic, often in the form of major fast-moving depressions, this milder, cooler climate is carried well inland, gradually petering out in the face of the eastern continental weather systems. There is a group of species – such as the Grey Bush-cricket (*Platycleis*

Then there is the effect of salt. All coastal areas, and especially those exposed to strong inshore winds, have salty soil and air. Clearly, the closer you are to the sea, the higher the salt levels. Areas that are regularly inundated by the sea or fre-

quently drenched by waves, such as salt marshes and the lower parts of coastal cliffs, have a rather limited but specialized flora and fauna. A number of plants – the halophytes – have developed special mechanisms for surviving this high burden of salt, such as salt-excreting glands on the leaf surfaces and the production of special stress proteins that help deal with the salt. The problem is most acute in the hot, enclosed environments of lagoons along the Mediterranean coast, where high evaporation and low rainfall produce very salty conditions. Only a few plants, such as the glassworts (*Salicornia* and *Sarcocornia* spp.), can withstand this amount of salt. Inland, the effect is progressively less, and it is usually not far before the full complement of plants and animals can return to normal and the specialists disappear.

Intertidal Zones

Between the high-tide and low-tide levels there is a wonderful, incredibly diverse and productive region that moulds and defines the character of the coast that it lies alongside. It is in the Atlantic and English Channel where this zone is significant, of course, as the Mediterranean tidal amplitude is too small to allow such a zone to develop.

The difference in height between low and high tide in the Atlantic and English Channel varies, but is always consider-

able, reaching a maximum in France at Mont St Michel Bay, where the tidal amplitude is 14 m, though elsewhere it is more like 6–8 m. On a vertical cliff or harbour wall, this amounts to exactly that – 6–8 m – but on a gently shelving beach this height difference results in huge areas, as much as several kilometres wide, being exposed at the lowest low tides. This regime produces a very specific set of living conditions – any animal or plant that lives there must tolerate complete immersion in salt water, as well as a period exposed to the prevailing climate, which may include heavy rain, frost and hot sun. There is an entire community of organisms, many of which occur nowhere else, that are adapted to this environment.

Of course, there is a strongly marked gradient down the shore. The very lowest levels are only exposed at extreme low tides that occur perhaps just twice a year, so here there are more marine species. At the highest levels, species are exposed to the external conditions for much of the day, and have to be strongly adapted to avoid desiccation. There is almost always an obvious zonation of species up the shore, each living where it can survive best. In general, it has been shown that the upper limit of a species' growth is limited by its ability to survive des-

ABOVE Brent Geese, especially the dark-bellied subspecies, are abundant in the food-rich intertidal areas of Brittany.

iccation (and possibly frost in colder areas), whereas its lower limit is defined by competition with other species. In other words, the lowest levels are much more favourable to a range of different species.

In rocky areas the zoning is often quite obvious, and many of the plants and animals can be clearly seen. In muddy areas, however, the distinctions at the surface are not quite so clear, though the amount of life in these three-dimensional soft intertidal zones can be huge, mainly in the form of small invertebrates. The main component species are *Corophium* shrimps, which can occur at densities of up to 28,000 per sq m in summer, several species of *Hydrobia* snail at densities of up to 42,000 per sq m, tellins (a type of bivalve mollusc) such as *Macoma baltica* at up to 3,500 per sq m, and many others.

Collectively, these organisms form a huge feeding resource for birds, especially waders, which remains available for much of the winter. This is one of the reasons why vast numbers of waders can be found along the northern and western coasts of France, both at passage periods and through the winter. The other is often the presence of one of the few marine flowering plants, the eelgrasses (*Zostera* spp.), which can be abundant in vast, dark-green intertidal swards on more stable mudflats. These are a staple food for some species of waterfowl, especially the dark-bellied subspecies of Brent Goose (*Branta bernicla bernicla*), which can be abundant in winter on the coasts of northern France.

The intertidal areas are also particularly important for fish, especially in relatively sheltered areas. They are the main nursery area for certain fish such as Plaice (*Pleuronectes platessa*), Dab (*P. limanda*), Flounder (*P. flesus*) and Sole (*Solea solea*), as well as many others, and a huge range of fish feed within this warm, productive intertidal zone.

A BRETON ROCKPOOL

Rockpools are wonderful places, glimpses into a marine world from which we are largely excluded, yet accessible and beautiful. Brittany, the north-western part of France, projects far out into the clean waters of the Atlantic, and it has a particularly rich marine flora and fauna. On rocky shores that shelve gently towards the sea, there are almost always rockpools – areas of water of varying size and depth that are submerged every day by the sea, but do not dry out between high tides. In general, the lower down the shore they are, the more diverse they will be, though if making a visit you also have to consider questions of visibility, access and safety. It is always worth checking when the really low tides will occur (usually a day or two after the full moon, with the very lowest in spring and autumn) so that you can get to the rockpools that are only occasionally exposed. Some good places for rockpools include the area around Roscoff (where there is also an interesting and unusual discovery centre specializing in seaweeds), west of Brest, and the Ile Grande area near Perros-Guirec.

Here is a typical Breton rockpool. There are seaweeds in plenty: green algae such as the aptly named Sea Lettuce (*Ulva lactuca*) and the curious gut-like *Enteromorpha intestinalis,* brown algae – particularly the wracks (*Fucus* spp.) and possibly the beautiful little Peacock's Tail (*Padina pavonia*), looking more like a piece of avant-garde pottery than an alga. The pinkish-red incrustations on the edge of the pool and underwater are one of the encrusting algae, most often *Lithophyllum encrustans*. Around the edge, often both above and below the water level, there are shells, usually closed up for the dry period – conical, pointed top-

BELOW Bladderwrack, one of the many brown algae (seaweeds) that occur around rockpools in the intertidal zone.

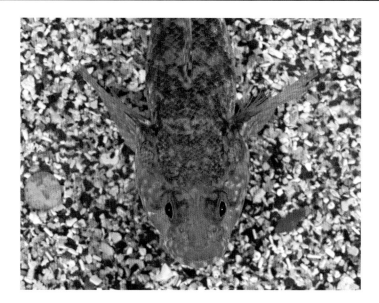

ABOVE Rock Gobies lay their eggs on the shore, usually on the underside of a rock or overhang, and they are guarded by the male.

shells such as the beautifully marked Painted Topshell (*Calliostoma zizyphinum*), the distinctive and familiar periwinkles like the edible Common Periwinkle (*Littorina littorea*) and perhaps a cluster of blue-black Common Mussels (*Mytilus edulis*). There are barnacles of course (for example *Balanus* spp.), though identifying individual species of these may be difficult. The larger limpets (*Patella* spp.) are probably there in serried ranks. At high tide they move off to feed on algae on the rocks, returning before they are exposed to their own 'parking place', which they have ground out of the rock.

Among the other immobile creatures, there are probably some sea anemones, such as the Strawberry Anemone (*Actinia fragacea*), with its bright red body dotted with red,

BELOW The aptly named Strawberry Anemone is common in many clean mid-shore rockpools.

the common Beadlet Anemone (*A. equina*) and the Snakelocks Anemone (*Anemonia viridis*), which has waving greenish-pink tentacles.

The more active creatures may take a little more finding, and it is best to approach a suitable pool slowly and quietly. There are almost certain to be a few blennies, such as the Common Blenny or Shanny (*Lipophrys pholis*), and some gobies, like the Rock Goby (*Gobius niger*), all small, active fish up to 12 cm long, with one or two dorsal fins.

Crabs are usually common, hiding in crevices or moving between stones if they feel secure. The Common Shore Crab (*Carcina maenas*) is abundant everywhere, a familiar greenish or brownish species up to about 7 cm across. Porcelain crabs are not scarce, but they are harder to spot as they are much smaller, like the Long-clawed Porcelain Crab (*Pisidia longicornis*), which is only a centimetre or so across its smooth, porcelain-like carapace; these are not true crabs, though they look rather like them, but are more closely related to lobsters.

Shrimps or prawns such as the large Rock Prawn (*Palaemon serratus*) are common, though easily missed as they can be almost transparent at times. Sometimes you may see long green worms moving slowly around on the bottom of the pool, or appearing from under seaweed. These are Green Leaf Worms (*Eulalia viridis*), up to 15 cm long with 100 or more segments, each bearing little paddle-like legs. Before you leave, check the surface of the water of the pool – here you will often find a tiny slate-blue insect only a few millimetres long, but conspicuous because it is found in groups of half a dozen or more. This is the springtail *Anurida* (or *Lipura*) *maritima*, one of the few insects to take to the sea. When the tide comes in, it usually creeps into a crevice to avoid being washed out to sea.

BELOW A Rock Prawn edges its way across the gravelly bottom of a rockpool.

Some Coastal Habitats

There are some special habitats, apart from the intertidal areas, that are almost exclusively confined to the coast. These include salt marshes, sand dunes, brackish lagoons and sea cliffs, though the cliffs are not necessarily very different from inland cliffs. Much of the diversity of habitats, especially the 'soft' habitats, is a product of the last ice age.

At the peak of the Ice Age, about 18,000 years ago, the sea level was about 130 m lower than it is now due to the huge amount of water locked up in the ice caps – an astonishing figure, made even more extraordinary by the difference it made to the outline of the coasts of France and elsewhere. Islands were joined to each other and to the mainland (including Britain and France, then joined by a wide band of land), and the whole coastline was everywhere further out to 'sea' than it is now, frequently by 100 km or more.

As the sea level steadily rose again towards the present-day levels, the continuing invasion of the land produced huge amounts of material – sand, gravel, pebbles and so on – that was constantly moved around and redeposited. The sea level rises more or less ceased about 3,000 years ago (apart from the very recent rises due to the current global warming), and the supply of new material has been reduced, but the present form of the coasts was determined by this episode. The vast areas of dunes, the silty salt marshes and the material that led to the for-

ABOVE Sand dunes and river estuary in the Courant d'Huchet reserve, on the coast of Les Landes.

mation of lagoons all derive from this period, and the courses of many rivers were altered to form new estuaries or deltas during this time.

Sand Dunes

There are huge areas of sand dune around the French coasts, to be found almost everywhere. They are formed by sand blowing inland and gradually becoming stabilized as soil develops and vegetation establishes. In some areas, like Les Landes, south of Bordeaux, the sand dunes stretch far inland, though nowadays they are largely planted with conifers. In most areas they form a thin strip up to 2 km wide along the coast with, generally, the unstable bare dunes towards the sea, and the increasingly stable dunes inland, covered by grass and often eventually forest.

Pure sand dunes are usually rather acidic, but often the sand is mixed with greater or lesser quantities of ground-up shells – almost pure calcium carbonate. This gives the dunes a quite different character, and the grassland is more like limestone grassland. In larger dune systems there are often areas of wetland – known as dune slacks – which may be open water, seasonal or otherwise, or just damp marshland or fen. They add immeasurably to the diversity of the dunes, and many

ABOVE The striking Sea Daffodil flowers at the hottest and driest time of year on otherwise bare southern sand dunes.

ABOVE A female Redshank guards her day-old chicks at their nest in a coastal salt marsh.

species particularly favour these areas. In very large dune areas these lakes can be very large, such as the string of lakes just inland down the south-western French coast from the mouth of the Gironde as far as Bayonne near the Spanish border.

Sand dunes are fascinating places for the naturalist. The flora is often very rich, with a mixture of widespread grassland species such as Ladies' Bedstraw (*Galium verum*) and many orchids, and specialized dune plants such as the Sea Holly (*Eryngium maritimum*), Sea Spurge (*Euphorbia paralias*), the joint-pine *Ephedra distachya*, Wild Asparagus (*Asparagus officinalis*), Jersey Thrift (*Armeria arenaria*) and many others. There are often rarities confined to limited areas, including the little sand toadflax *Linaria thymifolia* and the Dune Hawkweed (*Hieracium eriophorum*). In warmer parts the beautiful Sea Daffodil (*Pancratium maritimum*) is often abundant, producing its large, fragrant white flowers in the hottest part of summer.

There are special invertebrates, too, that do well on the dunes, including the two tiger beetles *Cicindela maritima* and *C. germanica*, and the distinctive snail *Theba pisana* that can be seen aestivating (passing the dry period of summer closed up to prevent desiccation) in vast quantities on duneland plants. Many more widespread species do very well on dunes, including the lovely Dark Green Fritillary (*Argynnis aglaja*) and

several burnet moths (*Zygaena* spp.). Natterjack Toads (*Bufo calamita*), though not confined to dunes, become increasingly dependent on dune-slack pools the further north you go.

Salt Marshes

These are partly an intertidal habitat, but rather like dunes they can mature and develop into coastal grassland at their upper edges. They are fascinating places, though dominated by rather few plants including the salt marsh grasses (*Spartina* spp.), the glassworts, and many oraches (*Atriplex* spp.) and goosefoots (*Chenopodium* spp.) – mostly members of the very salt-tolerant goosefoot family, Chenopodiaceae. There are patches of colour, too, including the pretty mauve and yellow flowers of the Sea Aster (*Aster tripolium*) and pink-flowered Sea Milkwort (*Glaux maritima*). Salt marshes are important feeding areas for plant-eating ducks such as the Pochard (*Aythya ferina*) and Wigeon (*Anas penelope*), and if undisturbed may be valuable nesting areas for waders such as the Redshank (*Tringa tetanus*).

Lagoons

Lagoons are shallow lakes located close to the coast, usually separated from the sea by a narrow strip of mud, shingle or sand, and interconnected with the water of the sea by channels

ABOVE The lagoon at St Cyprien, near Perpignan, is now protected as an important nature reserve.

or other means. They are therefore almost always saline to a degree, though the salinity depends on the amount of freshwater input and the speed of interchange with the sea water, and there are likely to be seasonal and diurnal changes.

In France, lagoons are best developed along the coast of the Mediterranean; here there is a long line of lagoons between Perpignan and Marseille, and there are more on the east coast of Corsica. There are few natural lagoons on the Atlantic coasts, though many artificial and semi-artificial ones exist, resulting from the salt industry or fishing, or created for nature conservation reasons. Whatever their origins, they tend to have rich and varied fish populations, and are often home to significant fishing and shellfish-rearing industries.

Shallow lagoons, especially if protected from too much fishing and hunting, as is the case in the Camargue, are wonderful feeding areas for water birds, especially ducks, some

waders and Greater Flamingoes (*Phoenicopterus ruber*), feeding on plants that include stoneworts (*Chara* spp.), and invertebrates, especially the highly productive Brine Shrimp (*Artemia parthenogenetica*), which can reach enormous densities in late winter.

Fish in Lagoons

The warm, shallow, productive saline waters of coastal lagoons are ideal places for fish. Some are resident, some visit just to feed, and others use the lagoons primarily as spawning grounds. A good lagoon might easily have 20 or more species of fish.

Mullets are especially noticeable large, slender, greyish fish that frequently feed near the surface. There are several rather similar species that commonly occur in lagoons, frequently in large numbers. They include the Thick-lipped Grey Mullet (*Crenimugil labrosus*), which can grow to almost 70 cm, the slightly smaller Thin-lipped Grey Mullet (*Liza ramada*) and the Golden Mullet (*L. aurata*). The Sand Smelt (*Atherina presbyter*) is a related but much smaller fish that can be found in shoals,

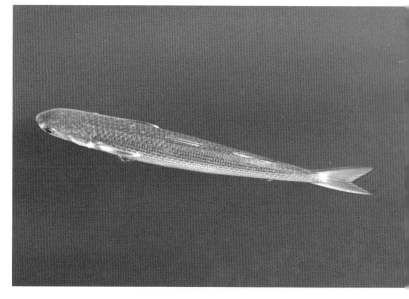

especially in summer when it enters lagoons to spawn. The pipefish are curious and distinctive fish, all sharing the characteristic of long, thin, flexible bodies protected by bony rings, and a snout-like head. The Great Pipefish (*Syngnathus acus*) is quite common in the southern lagoons. Flatfish such as the Turbot (*Psetta maxima*), Brill (*Scophthamnus rhombus*), Common Sole (*Solea solea*) and European Plaice (*Pleuronectes platessa*) are all common, and they are all popular target species for fisheries.

The Garfish (*Belone belone*) is a highly distinctive fish in the needlefish group, with a long, narrow, silvery body up to almost 1 m long, and a long, pointed beak armed with teeth. It

TOP, RIGHT A grey mullet swimming through the shallow waters of a lagoon. These fish 'hoover' fine silt layers from rocky surfaces, as well as feeding at the surface on plankton debris and algae scum.

CENTRE, RIGHT The Spotted Goby can be common in coastal lagoons.

BOTTOM, RIGHT Adult eels, such as this large individual, regularly visit coastal lagoons and estuaries to feed.

is a migrant that comes inshore in summer to feed on crustaceans and small fish in the lagoons and elsewhere. Other species include European Eels (*Anguilla anguilla*), gobies such as the Common Goby (*Potamoschistus microps*), Three-spined Sticklebacks (*Gasterosteus aculeatus*) and some gurnards.

One other fish should be mentioned here – the Mosquito Fish (*Gambusia affinis*). This little fish is a native of the Gulf of Mexico, but has been widely introduced throughout the warmer parts of the world as an agent of mosquito control. It is now thought to be the most widespread fish in the world, and is remarkably tolerant of high salinity, high temperatures, low oxygen levels and other difficult circumstances. There is an increasingly prevalent view that its introduction is a bad thing due to its impact on native aquatic ecosystems. It is common in the Camargue (where its failure to control mosquito numbers is all too clear!) and other similar sites in France.

Some Coastal Sites of Special Interest

An anti-clockwise tour around the coasts of France, from the Belgian border to Corsica, reveals a number of special sites, and here are a few that are of international importance. The Somme Estuary, or Baie de Somme, north-west of Abbeville, is

BELOW Beautiful salt marsh and mudflats in the Près-Salés nature reserve at the northern point of the Bassin d'Arcachon.

an internationally important coastal wetland, with a Ramsar site (see page 98) covering 170 sq km of superb salt marsh, dunes and other coastal habitats, visited by huge numbers of birds especially in winter. Further west, on either side of the Cherbourg Peninsula, there are huge important wetlands in each 'armpit'. On the eastern side, the Baie de Veys covers 370 sq km of mixed habitats, with enormous numbers of wintering and passage birds, while the even larger Mont St Michel Bay on the west side covers 640 sq km (of which about 220 sq km are mudflats!), accommodating tens of thousands of waders and waterfowl in winter or on migration.

Almost the whole of the Breton coast, from Mont St Michel round to Vannes, is attractive and of interest to the naturalist for its flowers, birds, insects and other life, but it is only possible here to mention a few highlights. The Sept-Iles off the north coast near Perros-Guirec hold the largest seabird colonies in France, and the whole area west of Vannes, comprising the Golfe du Morbihan and the Quiberon Peninsula, is wonderful for wintering and passage birds, dune flowers, insects and much else in a lovely matrix of salt marshes, mudflats, dunes, cliffs and terrestrial habitats.

South of St Nazaire, the coast is generally low-lying and sandy, with many areas of dunes, and important wintering bird areas at the Baie de Bourgneuf, sheltered by the Ile de Noirmoutier, and the Anse de L'Aiguillon, just north of La Rochelle. Both areas contain an enormous extent of mudflats

and salt marshes. From the mouth of the Gironde southwards to the Spanish border, the coast is dominated by west-facing beaches backed by dunes and forests, and an abundance of large dune slack lakes.

One site that stands out is the Dune du Pilat, just south-west of Arcachon. This is the highest dune in Europe, with a height that regularly exceeds 100 m (and has reached 117 m) in a dune that is about 500 m wide and several kilometres long, containing an estimated 60 million cubic metres of sand. It is also an interesting site for the naturalist, with a good flora in the more stable parts. The Bassin d'Arcachon, or Arcachon Bay, is itself an impressive site for birds, especially in winter, and the Ornithological Park at Teich is a good place from which to enjoy it.

The Mediterranean coast commences at the Spanish border at Cap Cerbère, where France's premier marine reserve is situated, covering 6.5 sq km of sea between Cerbère and Banyuls. The coast itself is not of particular interest, but the marine reserve is extremely species rich, noted for its corals, seahorses, fan mussels and a total of over 500 invertebrate species, as well as many species of fish.

From Argelès northwards and eastwards, the coast is characterized by a long string of lagoons, with occasional headlands such as Cap Leucate (excellent for migrating birds) and Le Cap d'Agde. The largest of these lagoons is the Bassin de Thau (or Etang de Thau), which is about 21 km long and 8 km wide, with an area of over 70 sq km, making it the second largest natural lake in France. It is a good area for flamingoes and all the other wildlife associated with lagoons, though it is rather heavily used as a fishing resource.

Eastwards, the Camargue is undoubtedly the premier coastal site in Mediterranean France, with its wonderful range of habitats and exceptional wildlife (see page 105). Further east, just east of Toulon, the Port-Cros National Park (part of the Iles d'Hyères) is a fascinating though small, protected area, with some fine relict fragments of Mediterranean vegetation and an impressive list of reptiles, including three gecko species and the endemic Tyrrhenian Frog (see Chapter 7).

The final stop on this short tour is Corsica. It would be fair to say that much the greater part of the coast of Corsica is of interest to the naturalist, being remarkably unspoiled and generally warm and beautiful. A few prime coastal sides stand out: on the north-west coast, the Scandola Peninsula is a large, protected, roadless area, a nature reserve and a World Heritage

ABOVE The dramatic pinnacles known as Les Calanches on the west coast of Corsica, just south of the Scandola Peninsula.

Site, with over 600 species of flowering plant, most of the special Corsican reptiles and amphibians (see Chapter 7), six species of bat, many interesting birds including three or four pairs of breeding Ospreys (*Pandion haliaetus*) and much else. The southern tip of Corsica is very different from the rest of the island, with beautiful limestone cliffs southwards from Bonifacio (where there is a rich flora and many breeding birds), and a large part-marine reserve around the Iles Lavezzi. This is a lovely unspoiled area, with large populations of some of the special Mediterranean seabirds and notably rich marine fauna and flora. On the more sheltered and softer east coast, there are several lagoons. These include the Etang de Biguglia, the largest and most important of them, and now protected as a National Nature Reserve.

Chapter 4
THE FLORA OF FRANCE

As you might expect from such a large, varied and well-connected country, the flora of France is enormous. Including Corsica, there are at least 4,900 native species of flowering plant in France, plus many hundreds of introduced non-native species, taking the list to a little over 6,000. In addition there are thousands of lichens, mosses, liverworts and fungi (the last of which, though taxonomically distinct from plants, are included here for convenience). Although not as large as the more southerly European countries of Spain, Italy or even Greece, the flora of France is nonetheless substantial and wonderfully varied, and constitutes about 40 per cent of the European flora. Almost every department has a flora of at least 1,200 species, equivalent to the total flora of some of Europe's less biodiverse countries, such as Denmark and Ireland. Perhaps surprisingly, the study of French plants is somewhat hampered by the fact that no complete flora of France exists in book form, either as a substantial reference work or as a simplified field guide, apart from reprints of historic works, which are not satisfactory on their own. Although work on such a flora is in progress, realistically it will be some time before it is published, which means that botanists have to rely on a series of regional and local floras, few of which are completely satisfactory.

LEFT A cornfield full of poppies, cornflowers and other plants on the western edge of the Alps.

On mainland France, excluding Corsica for the moment, there are relatively few truly endemic flowers. France is connected to other countries in almost every direction, and few species have evolved there in complete isolation. Therefore France shares a number of local endemics, for example with Italy in the alpine areas, and with Spain in the Pyrenees, but has relatively few of its own on the mainland. If you include all the shared endemics (also known as subendemics) that occur in France plus one or more neighbouring countries, though still nowhere else in the world, there are about 750 species – a high proportion of the flora – though if you exclude Corsica and restrict the list to just agreed mainland endemics, there are probably no more than 50 species.

It is always difficult to give a definite figure, as the differences between the French populations of a species and those of its nearest neighbours outside France may be quite small, so that some botanists make each a separate species, while others disagree. For example, one list of French endemic flowers lists nine different, mainly alpine tulips (*Tulipa* spp.) as being endemic to France, but few are listed in other floras, and only one, the Guillestre Tulip (*Tulipa platystigma*), is generally accepted as a genuine endemic species. Actually, this species has quite an interesting story, since it was discovered and described in 1855, but then forgotten and considered to be extinct. It was rediscovered near Guillestre (south of Briançon) in 1991, growing as a very small population in just one location. Plants are now being grown on in the garden of the nearby Maison de la Nature in the hope of propagating enough individuals to ensure that it has a more stable future.

The Massif Central is quite a centre of endemism in France because of its distinctive nature and isolation from the borders of any other country. If the mountains were higher, there would undoubtedly be many more endemics, as high-mountain specialists quickly become genetically isolated since there is little potential for intermediate populations to occur in the lowlands. Despite this limitation, there are a number of attractive and often quite distinctive endemics in this region.

Two species of ox-eye daisy are found on the limestone *causses*; these are rather similar to the common Ox-eye Daisy (*Leucanthemum vulgare*), though differing in distinct ways. *L. graminifolium* has narrow, almost grass-like leaves, and smallish flowers, whereas *L. subglaucum* has more oval leaves, greyish foliage and larger flowers that are 4–5 cm across. Both occur in dry, rocky calcareous places through much of the *causses* area. Another endemic plant of this limestone area is the attractive white-flowered Cévennes Saxifrage (*Saxifraga cebennensis*) (sometimes also written as *cevennensis*), which grows in flowery clumps on limestone or dolomite rock outcrops.

There are also two rather special endemic orchids that can be found in the limestone parts of the Massif Central: Aymonin's Orchid (*Ophrys aymoninii*) is a lovely brown- and yellow-flowered plant, most resembling a Fly Orchid (*O. insectifera*), though with many differences, including yellowish upper petals and a broad band of yellow across the lower lip, as well as having a different pollinator (see page 84). It is uncommon in grassland in the southernmost *causses*, though sometimes quite abundant where it does occur. The other species is the striking Aveyron Bee Orchid (*O. aveyronensis*), which is similar to many of the spider orchids, with a bold combination of purplish sepals and petals, and a large, furry brown lip. This is a rare and threatened plant found mainly on the Causse de Larzac in limestone grasslands, where it is undoubtedly declining despite a degree of legal protection.

A few endemics occur down the west coast of France, sufficiently isolated from other countries to have evolved alone. The attractive borage-relative *Omphalodes littoralis* is probably the most widespread and distinctive. This short, grey-leaved plant with abundant white flowers grows on dunes and other sandy habitats from Brittany southwards. Other coastal endemics here include the carrot *Daucus gadecaei* (confined to Brittany) and the asphodel *Asphodelus arrondeaui*, as well as a few plants shared with Spain such as the milk-vetch *Astragalus bayonensis*.

Of course the high mountains, the Alps and Pyrenees, are the greatest centres of endemism, though as noted above, most of the species that have evolved here are shared with adjacent countries. In the Alps as a whole there are hundreds of endemics, but only a few are confined solely to France. The pretty golden- or yellow-flowered Dauphine Cinquefoil (*Potentilla delphinensis*) is wholly French, growing mainly in the high areas of the Ecrins National Park. Though rather similar to several other cinquefoils, recent research has shown that it is quite distinct and does not interbreed with other species. Some species are just shared with the adjacent area of the nearest country. They include two attractive and rather similar alpine fritillaries, *Fritillaria tubiformis* and *F. involucrata*, which occur in the southern French Alps and over the border into Italy, but nowhere else.

Types of Flora

The origins and affinities of the flora of France are many and varied, with a wonderful mixture of northern, eastern, southern and western species. Some species, such as the Tree Spurge (*Euphorbia dendroides*), are essentially African, at the northern edge of their range in southern France, while others are primarily boreal, such as the Bog Arum (*Calla palustris*), which just

SOME ENDEMIC FRENCH FLOWERS, CLOCKWISE FROM THE TOP, LEFT
The Aveyron Bee Orchid is one of the rarest and most beautiful of French endemic plants; the pretty white-flowered *Omphalodes littoralis* is an endemic confined to parts of the Atlantic coast of France; this attractive alpine fritillary, *Fritillaria tubiformis*, is a subendemic that is confined to alpine areas along the French–Italian border; the lovely Dauphine Cinquefoil is a distinctive species found only in a small part of the French Alps.

creeps southwards into north-eastern France, and so on. The vast majority of French flowers come from a dozen or so families, as follows:

Family	No. of species
Asteraceae (Compositae): dandelions	757
Poaceae (Graminaceae): grasses	496
Fabaceae (Leguminosae): legumes	411
Rosaceae: roses	329
Brassicaceae (Cruciferae): cress	297
Caryophyllaceae: pinks	224
Scrophulariaceae: foxgloves	224
Apiaceae (Umbelliferae): carrots	204
Lamiaceae (Labiatae): deadnettles	185
Cyperaceae: sedges	183
Ranunculaceae: buttercups	165
Orchidaceae: orchids	approx. 140

Of the remaining familes, 48 only have a single species, and more than 100 have five or fewer species.

It is worth looking at a couple of the smaller families in greater detail to see how they are represented in France. The buttercup family, Ranunculaceae, is an extraordinarily varied group, so much so that it is often hard to see how its members could be related to each other, though recent genetic work has confirmed many of the earlier relationships. They range from simple small buttercups (*Ranunculus* spp.) and the pretty little Hepatica (*Hepatica nobilis*) to long-spurred columbines (*Aquilegia* spp.), climbing woody *Clematis* spp., and the petal-less meadow rues (*Thalictrum* spp.). There is no single linking feature, but in general they have spirally arranged leaves without stipules, and produce flowers that turn into a head of achenes (dry, one-seeded fruits) or follicles (dry, many-seeded fruits splitting along one side). Often the number of petals is variable, and in many species the sepals are more highly coloured and larger than the petals, for instance in the anemones (*Anemone* spp.).

The Marsh Marigold (*Caltha palustris*) and Globe Flower (*Trollius europaeus*) are two rather similar species, both widespread in France. The Marsh Marigold or Kingcup is common virtually throughout the country in wet meadows, though the further south you go, the more it is confined to mountain areas. Its beautiful deep yellow or orange, cup-shaped flowers light up many a landscape in spring. The Globe Flower has paler yellow, more enclosed flowers, and is more of a mountain flower everywhere, occurring commonly in mid-altitude meadows, especially on limestone.

The hellebores are rather less striking, and the flowers are dominated by their usually greenish sepals. The Stinking Hellebore (*Helleborus foetidus*) occurs very widely on limestone, in woods, pastures and even rocky outcrops, and especially in mountain areas, while the Green Hellebore (*H. viridis*) is more secretive, rather rarer and absent from many of the drier parts of the country. Corsica has its own species – *H. argutifolius* – which is widespread on the island and often grown elsewhere in gardens for its early flowering. The Baneberry or Herb Christopher (*Actaea spicata*) is an attractive plant, with spikes of clustered white flowers rising from deeply divided leaves, eventually maturing into black berries. It can be found mainly in hill or mountain areas, especially in the east and usually on limestone or other lime-rich soils.

The monkshoods and larkspurs *Aconitum*, *Delphinium* and *Consolida* form a distinctive group, with a number of species in France. Wolfsbane (*Aconitum lycoctonum*) produces tall spikes of pale yellow, hairy flowers in mountain meadows, all having the typical monkshood shape in which the upper two sepals form a tall hood that encloses the larger nectaries. The Common Monkshood (*A. napellus*) has similar but

BELOW Seguier's Buttercup, a pretty white-flowered species found mainly on high limestone screes.

ABOVE A fine clump of the gorgeous Alpine Pasque Flower in its white form, growing in high pastures in the Alps.

ABOVE The Common Pasque Flower is widespread in France, growing especially on the limestones of the north and west of the country.

larger flowers that are a deep violet-blue, and the Variegated Monkshood (*A. variegatum*) has paler blue flowers streaked with white. All occur mainly in the mountains.

The perennial larkspurs, all in the genus *Delphinium*, are beautiful stately plants, closely related to the garden plants of the same name. There are several species in France, all blue, with larger, more open flowers than the monkshoods, a long spur behind and no hood. The Mountain Larkspur (*D. montanum*) is a plant of high meadows and stony places in the Pyrenees, while the rather similar *D. dubium* occurs in the Maritime Alps, and the Alpine Larkspur (*D. elatum*) can be found throughout the alpine area. There are also several species of annual larkspur, now in the genus *Consolida*, which tend to be plants of cornfields and waste places, such as the slender and attractive Forking Larkspur (*C. regalis*).

The anemones are an important group of flowers in France, often dominant where they do occur. In all the species, it is the sepals that form the main petal-like structures, so if you look under the flowers you will see that there are no green sepals

on the outside – this can often help to distinguish them from the similar buttercups or other genera. Wood Anemones (*Anemone nemorosa*) are familiar and widespread, but two similar species are much more local. The Snowdrop Windflower (*A. sylvestris*) is a large, erect plant, with showy white flowers up to 7 cm across, made up of only five sepals; it is uncommon in the eastern mountain areas of France. The Trifoliate Anemone (*A. trifolia*) is rather like the Wood Anemone, but with distinctly three-lobed leaves, and is much rarer, found mainly in mountain woods. A particularly striking plant of mountain grasslands throughout France is the Narcissus-flowered Anemone (*A. narcissiflora*); despite having a quite different structure, the clusters of white flowers do somehow resemble a narcissus, especially from a distance. The Yellow Wood Anemone (*A. ranunculoides*) is quite different, with rich golden-yellow flowers on low-growing plants, often forming carpets in deciduous woodland.

Pasque flowers (*Pulsatilla* spp.) are generally similar to the anemones (and used to be included in the same genus), but

have fruits with long, feathery styles, collectively forming a conspicuous globular seedhead. The Common Pasque Flower (*P. vulgaris*) has pretty nodding, purplish-blue flowers, usually only a few centimetres high, and it is widespread in calcareous grasslands from the Belgian border to the southern *causses*. The Cévennes Pasque Flower (*P. rubra*) is similar, but taller with more wine-red flowers. There are several mountain specialists, most notably the Alpine Pasque Flower (*P. alpina*), a tall species with erect flowers that may be white or yellow, depending on the subspecies, and the Spring Pasque Flower (*P. vernalis*), a low-growing plant with large flowers that are white inside and purplish outside. All its parts are covered with long, silky hairs, and it flowers very early as soon as (or occasionally before) the snow melts from the pastures.

In France, the genus *Clematis* has a number of rather undistinguished species in the wild (most of the cultivated species originated in Asia), except for the beautiful Alpine Clematis (*Clematis alpina*). This is a scrambling or climbing plant, like most clematis, but it produces large solitary, nodding, blue-purple flowers with four petal-like sepals. It is found in alpine areas in eastern France, especially on acid soil.

The Yellow Pheasant's Eye (*Adonis vernalis*) is a striking plant growing in large clumps up to 50 cm high, covered with large, anemone-like yellow flowers in spring. It is an uncommon species, now legally protected, to be found at its best on the limestone *causses*, with outliers in the hilly parts of east France. There is a similar endemic species in the Pyrenees, the Pyrenean Pheasant's Eye (*A. pyrenaica*), with smaller flowers

ABOVE The marvellous Cévennes Pasque Flower showing both its wine-red flowers and feathery fruits.

BELOW A clump of Alpine Clematis clambering over trees and shrubs to get to the light.

(up to 4 cm across), which grows in rocky places up to about 2,400 m. The remaining species of pheasant's eye are mainly annual and red-flowered, such as the widespread cornfield weed Pheasant's Eye (*A. annua*). The defining genus of the buttercup family is, of course, the buttercup genus (*Ranunculus* spp.). There are dozens of species in France, too many to mention here, though it is worth stating that they split roughly into the yellow-flowered species – including very widespread species such as the Meadow Buttercup (*R. acris*); the white-flowered aquatic species known as the water-crowfoots, like the River Water-crowfoot (*R. fluitans*), one of the species that may fill a river from bank to bank with a heady mass of white flowers in early summer; and the white-flowered mountain species like the pretty, delicate Seguier's Buttercup (*R. seguieri*), found on high-altitude limestone screes, and the amazing Glacier Crowfoot, whose pinkish-tinged white flowers can be found at heights of over 4,000 m. There is no space to do more than just mention the love-in-a-mists (*Nigella* spp.), *Isopyrum* spp., *Hepatica* spp., the marvellous columbines, the Mousetail (*Myosurus minima*), and the feathery meadow rues – all are in the same family, yet all are rather different from each other.

ABOVE A wonderful plant of Lady's Slipper Orchid, perhaps the most beautiful and elusive of all the orchids of France.

The Orchids

These plants, all members of the Orchidaceae, are many people's favourite flowers, though for others they are too showy, or too diverse and confusing a group. There is no doubt, though, that they include some beautiful flowers, with an added indefinable cachet that goes beyond their mere beauty. Finding orchids is always a pleasure, and finding an abundance of species together is a real excitement. For the orchid-lover, France is a very special place; this is particularly true of the southern half of the country, where there is a vast range of species to be found. It is hard to define the number of species in France precisely, because a good deal of research is still going on in the orchid group and species are constantly being redefined, but there are at least 135 species, and more likely over 140, all of which are terrestrial.

Perhaps the premier species, both taxonomically (for it is the only representative of its subfamily in France) and because of its beauty, is the Lady's Slipper Orchid (*Cypripedium cal-*

ABOVE A clump of Long-spurred Orchid growing on the limestone near Bonifacio in the far south of Corsica.

ABOVE Military Orchids are widespread and common in France wherever there are grassy pastures on limestone.

ceolus). It is a quite astonishing species to find in the wild, with its masses of very large (up to 7 cm across), purple and yellow flowers, each with a hollow, slipper-like lip, and the excitement of finding it in the wild never palls, however many times you see it. It is an undoubtedly rare species overall, essentially confined to hilly areas and lower mountains, almost always on limestone, though it is not uncommon in parts of the Vercors, the pre-alpine ranges and the Alps.

The marsh orchids (*Dactylorhiza* spp.) are quite different. There are many of them, though all share the characteristics of dense spikes of usually purple flowers with long, leafy bracts among them, often hollow stems, divided finger-lobed tubers and a general preference for wet places. They are a rather promiscuous group, with a strong tendency towards hybridization, which can make certain identification a tricky process. One of the most distinctive and attractive of the marsh orchids is the Elder-flowered Orchid (*D. sambucina*), which occurs in two colour forms – one with rich yellow flowers dotted and suffused with red, and the other with reddish-purple flowers,

though there is always a hint of yellow in the centre. This is really a mountain plant, common in all the upland regions, especially on acid soils. A closely related but much rarer species is *D. insularis*, which is confined to the Pyrenees and Corsica within France.

There are a dozen or so other marsh orchids, including the endemic *D. brennensis*, which is confined to the Brenne area, though not all experts agree that it is distinct from the closely related Tall Marsh Orchid (*D. elata*). The spotted orchids are similar – in the same genus, but with generally paler and more lilac-pink flowers.

The genus *Orchis* contains many of the most familiar French orchids. They differ from the marsh orchids in having round tubers and no leaf-like bracts in the inflorescence, among other things, though it should be mentioned that this whole genus is in a state of flux because DNA analysis is producing conflicting evidence as to the affinities of various species. Early Purple Orchids (*O. mascula*) are probably the most widespread of all orchids in France. Their elegant tall,

ABOVE A close-up view of a flower of the Lady Orchid, showing the skirt and bonnet of the 'lady'.

ABOVE The Lizard Orchid is the strangest of all French orchids, with its long, wavy lip rather resembling a lizard's tail.

deep reddish-purple spikes are found in a range of habitats, from lowland woodlands to high alpine meadows, and it is hardly surprising that a number of subspecies or closely allied species have been distinguished, such as the stately *O. langei*, an Iberian species that reaches into the French Pyrenees. The Green-winged Orchid (*O. morio*) can look like an Early Purple Orchid from a distance, but is usually shorter and a duller purple with strong green veins on the lateral sepals.

A particularly striking member of the *Orchis* group is the Long-spurred Orchid (*O. longicornu*), with richly coloured flowers and a long, upturned spur. Within France, it is confined to Corsica, especially on the southern limestone. There is also a small group of lovely yellow-flowered members of the genus, including *O. pallens* (a mountain species) and the Provence Orchid (*O. provincialis*), a southern species.

There is a trio of *Orchis* species that holds a particular fascination for visitors from more northerly countries such as Britain, as all are particularly rare there, and all are rather beautiful. The Military Orchid (*O. militaris*) is a tall, stately

plant up to 60 cm high, with a spike of pinkish-red flowers, each shaped like a man with a helmet. The Monkey Orchid (*O. simia*) is rather similar, but the 'arms' and 'legs' of the lip are very narrow and look as though they have been dipped in dark red ink. The Lady Orchid (*O. purpurea*) has flowers with a broad, flared, skirt-like lip, and an attractive dark bonnet – it is easy to see where all their English names come from. All are widespread and locally common in France, especially towards the south, and most often on limestone.

The Lizard Orchid (*Himantoglossum hircinum*) is a one-off, the only species in its genus in France, with a very distinctive appearance. It is probably the tallest orchid, regularly reaching almost a metre high, with a dense spike of flowers, each with a very long, thin, wavy lip, up to 6 cm long (like a lizard's tail, hence the English name). Interestingly, its various French names, such as *orchis bouc*, all refer to its strong, goat-like odour, rather than to its appearance. It is widespread almost throughout France, though most common on the mid-southern limestones, where it can even be a dominant roadside plant.

ABOVE The Late Spider Orchid has some of the largest flowers of the genus *Ophrys*, pollinated by long-horned bees such as *Eucera longicornis*.

ABOVE Bee Orchids are widespread and common on calcareous soils almost throughout France.

Another distinctive group, with several species involved, is the tongue orchids. They are easy to recognize, with tightly clustered, greyish-pink sepals forming a hood, from which protrudes a large, usually tongue-shaped and often deep red lip – the 'tongue' of the English name – but the individual species may be hard to recognize. There are about eight species in France, including a Corsican subendemic, differing in details of lip shape, colour and so on.

The orchid genus that probably arouses the most passion, both positive and negative, is *Ophrys*, comprising the spider orchids and bee orchids. These orchids all have very beautiful flowers, sharing the characteristic of having a large, furry, swollen lower lip (a modified petal) and a number of other characters designed to attract hapless insects (see right). Southern Europe is the world epicentre for this genus, and there is a huge number of species spread across the continent, including many in France.

Unfortunately, these orchids have a tendency to produce vast numbers of slightly different forms, which may or may not be defined as stable species or subspecies, and it is here that the greatest passions are aroused. For the real enthusiast, this means that there are a vast number of different species or vari-

eties to be tracked down; for the less committed, it means that many of them are very hard to identify!

The pace of taxonomic change is probably now slowing down as more is known about the group, but there are still many anomalies and difficulties, and the latest edition of the orchidophile's bible, *Orchids of Europe* by Pierre Delforge, published in 2006, has many new names and species compared with its predecessor from five years before. With these provisos in mind, it is still possible to enjoy this group, and marvel at its strange beauty and fascinating habits.

Pseudocopulation and Insect Mimicry in the Genus *Ophrys*
The fascinating structure and great variety of flowers in the genus *Ophrys* is all geared to one aim: attracting insects to bring about pollination of the flowers. It is obvious enough from looking at the flowers of, say, a Fly Orchid, that they have evolved to look rather like an insect, often in quite fine detail – for example, the two upper petals of the Fly Orchid have been reduced to narrow brown structures just like the antennae of many insects, and the bluish-grey patch on the lower lip resembles the reflection from a pair of wings. What is less obvious is that the flowers also emit a cocktail of chemicals (up to

100 different ones have been found), some of which resemble the pheromones of certain insects.

The main pollinators for these orchids are members of the order Hymenoptera, which includes the bees and wasps, and in the solitary species the males tend to emerge before the females. When the females do emerge, they produce attractive scents wherever they go, which pull in the males from quite a distance. When the males initially emerge, there are likely to be no females, so these rather similar-looking flowers that also release the right scent prove highly attractive, and the males visit and attempt to mate with the flowers.

Due to the precise structure of the flower, the first male to visit leaves carrying two sacs of pollen (the pollinia), which have sticky pads at their bases to attach them to the insect's head. The male then visits another flower, where pollination is effected, though eventually the females emerge and the flowers lose their appeal.

It is interesting that almost all the species of *Ophrys* have just one species of insect, or occasionally two or three, that acts as its pollinator. In other words, the flowers have evolved quite precisely in both appearance and scent to attract that specific insect – but this is not co-evolution, as the insect gets nothing from the arrangement. There is no nectar and no female – the males are lured in by an illusion, though it probably does them no harm, as they do not lose their interest in real females when these eventually appear.

This is clearly a finely balanced system, and in some instances it has broken down, especially where plants are at the edge of the range. For example, in core areas, including much of France, the Fly Orchid is quite successful in getting pollinated, whereas in Britain only a very small percentage of flowers is pollinated. The Bee Orchid has ceased using the method at all in many areas – presumably because it was failing – and self-pollination is the norm.

Some orchids and their pollinators include the following – all the insects listed are hymenopterans, mainly types of solitary bee.

Orchid	Pollinator
Fly Orchid (*O. insectifera*)	*Argogorytes mystaceus*
Aymonin's Orchid (*O. aymoninii*)	*Andrena combinata*
Sawfly Orchid (*O. tenthredinifera*)	*Eucera nigrilabi*
Late Spider Orchid (*O. fuciflora*)	*E. longicornis* + others
Woodcock Orchid (*O. scolopax*)	*E. interrupta*
Bee Orchid (*O. apifera*)	*Andrena hattorfiana*

ABOVE, RIGHT The flowers of the Fly Orchid are remarkably accurate insect mimics, with the two upper petals reduced to antennae-like spikes.
BELOW, RIGHT The Sawfly Orchid is an essentially southern species confined to the Mediterranean areas of France.

The Flowers of the Pyrenees

Apart from Corsica, perhaps, the Pyrenees have the most distinctive and special assemblage of flowers in France. Including the immediate Spanish side, the flora of the Pyrenees amounts to about 4,500 species, of which 160 are endemic to some degree, and many are of special beauty and interest. Generally speaking, it is the higher-altitude species that stand out as different, as they are more isolated from their nearest equivalent populations. Obviously, with this number of species involved, we can do no more than glance at the range of plants and give a hint of their variety, concentrating particularly on those that are confined to the Pyrenees.

The rock jasmines are glorious diminutive, cushion-like high-altitude specialists, in the primrose family Primulaceae, often covered with colourful flowers. There are nine species in the Pyrenees, including four that are endemic to the Pyrenees alone – *Androsace pyrenaica, A. cylindrica, A. hirtella* and *A. ciliata*, as well as the pretty Pink Rock Jasmine (*A. carnea*) that is endemic to several Western European mountain ranges. In the same family there is an endemic snowbell, the Pyrenean Snowbell (*Soldanella villosa*), quite similar to the more wide-

LEFT The Pink Rock Jasmine growing in high Pyrenean pastures near Gavarnie.

OPPOSITE, ABOVE Some of the high Pyrenean hay meadows, especially those in the Pyrenees National Park, are astonishingly flowery.

OPPOSITE, BELOW A mass of English Iris (*Iris xiphioides*) growing in a high Pyrenean pasture, pictured with the mist closing in.

BELOW One of the autumn-flowering crocuses, *Crocus nudiflorus*, is abundant in high Pyrenean pastures in September and October.

ABOVE The rare and beautiful Pyrenean Shrubby Gromwell growing high in the eastern Pyrenees.

BELOW The Pyrenean Ramonda is a very special Pyrenean plant, a rare survivor from a time when the climate was much warmer.

ABOVE Insectivorous Long-leaved Butterworts grow abundantly in wet rocky places in the Pyrenees, especially on calcareous cliffs.

BELOW The Pyrenean Poppy (*Papaver lapeyrousianum*) is an uncommon Pyrenean endemic.

spread Alpine Snowbell (*S. alpina*), which also occurs. Both have distinctive nodding, purplish-pink bells, which are heavily fringed at the edges, and both are noted for their habit of flowering as soon as the snow melts, or even flowering as they push up through it.

A dozen or more gentians (*Gentiana* spp.) occur in the Pyrenees, including many of the beautiful large, blue-trumpet species, and the widespread and distinctive Large Yellow Gentian (*Gentiana lutea*). There is an easily recognized, more violet-coloured species, the Pyrenean Gentian (*G. pyrenaica*), which is not endemic, and the rather less distinctive Pyrenean Trumpet Gentian (*G. occidentalis*), which is endemic to the Pyrenees and nearby Spanish mountains. A rather special and very rare shrub, which has slightly similar blue flowers and only occurs in a few places in the eastern Pyrenees, is the Shrubby Gromwell (*Lithodora oleifolium*), confined to a few limestone rock crevices.

One of the most interesting and attractive of plants in the Pyrenees is the Pyrenean Ramonda (*Ramonda pyrenaica*). It is a lovely species, with a rosette of crinkly leaves from which a number of large blue-purple flowers grow on long, leafless stems, quite common in woods and shady rocks at about 1,200–1,800 m, sometimes in abundance. It is particularly interesting in that it is the sole member in France of the gloxinia or African violet family (Gesneriaceae), and a relict of the flora of pre-Ice Age times that has somehow survived from when Europe was more African in its climate.

The Pyrenees range is probably the best place in Europe to see butterworts (*Pinguicula* spp.), a fascinating group of insectivorous plants. There are six species here, all sharing the characteristic rosette of smoothly sticky leaves, from which blue, white or purplish flowers arise on long, thin stalks. Small insects become trapped on the sticky leaves, and are digested by enzymes secreted from the leaf surface, then absorbed as a nutrient-rich broth. This allows the butterworts to grow in difficult places such as nutrient-poor wetlands and damp cliff faces. The Large-flowered Butterwort (*P. grandiflora*) is endemic to south-west Europe, and has distinctive large purplish flowers, while the Long-leaved Butterwort (*P. longifolia*) has pale blue flowers and long, pale green leaves. Two other special species are worth mentioning from among the many

ABOVE The Pyrenean Bellflower has masses of large pale blue flowers, and is common throughout the central Pyrenees.

contenders. The Pyrenean Columbine (*Aquilegia pyrenaica*) is a gorgeous plant, more slender than the Common Columbine (*A. vulgaris*) and producing just a few large blue-purple flowers on slender stems. It grows in crevices and rocky places on limestone up to about 2,500 m. Finally, the Pyrenean Bellflower (*Campanula speciosa*) is a striking and distinctive plant, erect, up to 60 cm high and bearing dozens of large, pale blue bell-flowers, each up to 5 cm long. It is endemic to the Pyrenees, Corbières and western Cévennes, where it grows in limestone crevices, screes and other rocky places.

The Special Plants of Corsica

Botanically, Corsica is a world apart. Geographically and eco-logically, it has more in common with mainland Italy and Sardinia than with France, and many of its species are more likely to be found in Italy than in France, though it also has much that is unique. The nearest part of mainland France is about 160 km away, mainland Italy 80 km and Sardinia only 12 km, so this comes as no surprise.

Due to its long-standing isolation from the mainland (it is about 5 million years since the Mediterranean reflooded after completely drying out), and relative freedom from glaciation, there has been ample time for species to evolve separately either exclusively to Corsica or shared with Sardinia and pos-sibly other islands. Those shared with Sardinia and/or other nearby islands are known as Tyrrhenian endemics, named after the Tyrrhenian Sea in which these islands lie.

There are about 2,500 species of native flower on Corsica, plus a large number of introduced species. Within this number, there are 296 endemic taxa (that is, including both species and finer subdivisions such as subspecies), of which 131 are con-fined to Corsica, 75 are shared with Sardinia, and 11 are shared with Sardinia and the Balearic Islands. These endemics come from a whole range of families, and some species are highly distinctive, while others are barely distinct from their nearest relatives.

Highlights include the very attractive Corsican Storksbill (*Erodium corsicum*), which has large, deep pink flowers and barely divided greyish leaves, and enough appeal to be quite commonly grown in gardens. Within Corsica, it occurs mainly in south-western coastal areas, for example around Bonifacio. Often growing with it is another endemic, the surprisingly del-icate cabbage-relative *Morisia monanthos*, which consists of a small rosette of shiny leaves with a little pile of almost stemless golden flowers in the centre. Another very distinctive species is the blue alkanet *Anchusa crispa*, which grows in sandy places on the coast and has pale or bright blue flowers, and distinc-tive bristly, wavy-edged leaves.

A number of bulbs and related plants do well on Corsica. Sand crocuses (*Romulea* spp.) are quite common in coastal areas around the Mediterranean, including those on Corsica, where there are four endemics as well as more widespread species. The endemics all have deep purplish flowers; *Romulea corsica* is a strict endemic, while *R. requienii*, *R. revelieri* and *R. ligustica* all also occur elsewhere.

There are two endemic crocuses, the tiny *Crocus minimus*, which flowers very early in the year in the lowlands, and the larger *C. corsicus*, which produces beautiful purplish-streaked

ABOVE, LEFT The daffodil relative *Pancratium illyricum* growing in abundance at the prehistoric site of Filitosa on Corsica.
BELOW, LEFT *Morisia monanthos*, a tiny cabbage relative, grows in rather sandy, open places, especially near the coast.

flowers, usually higher in the mountains in grasslands and open pine woodlands.

There are also several endemic or subendemic orchids on Corsica. Three members of the spider orchid group, *Ophrys morisii* (a lovely purple species), *O. conradiae*, which is very like the Woodcock Orchid (*O. scolopax*), and *O. panormitana* ssp. *praecox*, with paler greenish-pink sepals and petals, are not infrequent in the south, mainly on the limestone of the Bonifacio area. The Nuoro Tongue-orchid (*Serapias nurrica*) occurs mainly in damp, acidic pastures over granite. The most frequently seen of the endemic bulbs is the striking daffodil relative *Pancratium illyricum*, with clusters of large white flowers. It is widespread and does well in some of the popular visitor sites such as the prehistoric village of Filitosa. Finally, there are some lovely and distinctive high-altitude endemics, such as the Corsican Butterwort (*Pinguicula corsica*), with white flowers, two dwarf daisies, *Bellis bernardii* and *B. nivale*, a version of the Alpine Pasque Flower (*Pulsatilla alpina* ssp. *cyrnea*), a basil-thyme, *Acinos corsicus,* and many others.

The Alien Invaders

There are at least 1,000 species of non-native plant that have become common enough, and adapted enough, to be considered as a part of the French flora, though not necessarily a welcome one. Some are quite benign, and show few signs of spreading and ousting the native flora. Others are more aggressive: they may have found a niche not fully exploited by the native flora, or brought with them a powerful means of dispersing or dominating a habitat.

The Himalayan Balsam (*Impatiens glandulifera*) is now quite common in France in wet places, especially along rivers. To some extent, this plant uses an unfilled niche as it has a particular ability to spread along rivers and grow in the bare mud along the margins, where the river rises and falls. It has capsules that explode when ripe, hurling the water-resistant seeds into the water, where they soon spread to a potential new habitat. However, it also spreads readily out of this environment into adjacent wetland areas, and is frequently considered to be a problem.

One of the worst current problems is the invasion of waterways almost throughout France by a South American water primrose (though actually the population now appears to comprise two closely related species, *Ludwigia peploides* and *L. uruguayensis*). They were accidentally introduced into southwest France in the 1820s, and for a long while remained in that area. More recently, however, they have begun migrating northwards, and have now reached the Belgian border in the

ABOVE, RIGHT The purple-striped flowers of the endemic Corsican crocus *Crocus corsicus* growing high in the Corsican pinewoods.

BELOW, RIGHT The uncommon Corsican Storksbill is one of the most attractive species in its genus, also widely grown in gardens.

far north of France. They are very aggressive plants, growing quickly and establishing dense mats of vegetation where little else grows. Unfortunately, they are barely palatable to aquatic herbivores, and their presence can quickly lower the dissolved oxygen content, making the environment generally less suitable for aquatic animals, especially invertebrates. They also seem to be becoming increasingly frost tolerant, despite their tropical origins. The problem is serious enough for several research programmes to have been initiated, though no complete solution has yet been proposed.

This is probably the worst of the species currently invading France, but there are many others, including the Tree Groundsel (*Baccharis halimifolia*) from North America – known as *le cotonnier* in French because of its abundance of cottony seeds – which is becoming common on some south-western coastal habitats, and the False Acacia (*Robinia pseudoacacia*) that is now so abundant in many places in France.

The Lower Plants

Apart from the flowering plants and ferns, there are many other species of plant in France, most notably the mosses, liverworts and algae. Also discussed here are the unrelated but functionally similar fungi, and the lichens, which are symbiotic associ-

ABOVE An invading mass of South American Water Primroses taking over the wetlands of the Marais d'Orx Reserve.

ations of algae and fungi. Collectively, the list of these organisms amounts to many thousands of species, though their study is a specialized field and most people barely notice them.

Perhaps the most obvious and attractive of these groups is the lichens. Due to its diversity of habitats and climates, France has a wonderful range of lichens, especially in the moist, clean air of the Atlantic coastal zone and in the higher mountain areas. A good example of a coastal lichen is the beautiful golden *Teloschistes chrysothamnus*, which grows on Blackthorn twigs in mild, clean coastal areas from Normandy southwards, and is quite common in places. Particularly interesting is the fact that this species is now virtually extinct in the UK (although it has recently been rediscovered in Guernsey after 140 years), despite the existence of similar habitats in the same climatic zone. It shows how quite subtle climatic differences, and possibly differences in air quality, can make such a large difference to lichens.

A couple of mountain species are often noticed: the Tree Lungwort (*Lobaria pulmonaria*) grows prolifically on and around trees in areas such as the Vosges (though it may also be a coastal species elsewhere), and the striking Wolf Lichen

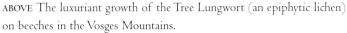

ABOVE The luxuriant growth of the Tree Lungwort (an epiphytic lichen) on beeches in the Vosges Mountains.

ABOVE, RIGHT The distinctive yellow fronds of Wolf Lichen growing on larches high in the French Alps.

RIGHT The spectacular orange lichen *Teloschistes chrysothamnus* grows on blackthorn bushes in particularly unpolluted areas along the coast, such as Brittany.

(*Letharia vulpina*) is a yellow, beard-like species often seen covering the bark of larches and other conifers at high altitudes. It gets its name from the fact that in North America, a concoction from its highly poisonous branches was used to kill wolves and foxes – or so it is said!

The bryophytes (mosses and liverworts) are comparatively poorly known in France, though there are at least 1,600 species. Some – like all the bog mosses – are protected by law due to their rarity, their role in bog formation and their sensitivity to air pollution.

Fungi have an important place in the hearts of the French people, since many fungi are edible and some, such as truffles, chanterelles and ceps, are regarded as really special delicacies. There are over 2,500 species of fungus in France; they are most common in woods everywhere, but are also found in grasslands, wetlands and even sand dunes.

Chapter 5

BIRD LIFE IN FRANCE

France is a wonderful country for both birds and birdwatchers, due to its central position in Europe, its wide range of habitats and the large area of remaining good bird habitats. Not only do hundreds of species breed in France, with many remaining as residents all year round, but many others pass through on their way from northern Europe or the Arctic regions to Africa or other wintering grounds. The total number of species recorded is well over 500 (depending, of course, on what records are accepted, which birds are considered to be native or naturalized, and so on), which is roughly two-thirds of all European species.

LEFT Cattle Egrets in breeding plumage feeding among cattle in a field of Purple Bugloss.

ABOVE The ancient Corsican Pine forest in the mountains of Corsica is a superb habitat for birds such as the endemic Corsican Nuthatch.

THE LIGUE POUR LA PROTECTION DES OISEAUX (LPO) has recently published an updated list of all birds officially recorded in France, with their current status, which gives a clear overview of the French avifauna. To give a further idea of the importance of France to European bird life, BirdLife International estimates that of the 162 bird species of European concern that breed regularly in France, six are of global concern. These are the Black Vulture (*Aegypius monachus*), which has been reintroduced into France, Lesser Kestrel (*Falco naumanni*), Corncrake (*Crex crex*), Little Bustard (*Tetrax tetrax*), Audouin's Gull (*Larus audouinii*) and Corsican Nuthatch (*Sitta whiteheadi*). Another species, the globally threatened Aquatic Warbler (*Acrocephalus paludicola*), passes through the country on migration.

Although the figures for birds in France are impressive overall, most of the six species that are of global concern are actually not faring very well in France. The Black Vulture has just a small number of reintroduced pairs, the Lesser Kestrel only exists in a small population in La Crau, and the Corncrake, Audouin's Gull and Little Bustard have all declined in recent years, severely in the case of the Little Bustard, which has been reduced to around 1,000 displaying males. The Corsican Nuthatch is France's only wholly endemic bird, discussed in more detail below. France also has a special importance for water birds, including non-breeding migrants, birds of prey, and birds of woodland, coast and mountain.

Corsica's Endemic Species

Metropolitan France has only one completely endemic bird, the Corsican Nuthatch. It is totally confined to the French island of Corsica, where it takes the place of the larger Common Nuthatch (*Sitta europaea*), which does not occur here, though it is common elsewhere in most of France. The Corsican Nuthatch is a distinctive bird, with a black cap, white eyebrow stripe and black stripe through the eye, and it is perhaps most similar to the eastern Mediterranean Krüper's Nuthatch (*Sitta krueperi*), though it lacks the red breast patch of the latter species.

On Corsica, this nuthatch is almost completely confined to the high forests of Corsican Pine (*Pinus nigra* subsp. *salzmannii* var. *corsicana*) – at least as a breeding bird – between the altitudes of 1,000 and 1,800 m. Optimal habitat for the bird is the oldest stands, which include many old trunks, dead wood and fallen timber, with plenty of suitable nesting sites. It is estimated that birds can reach a density of three or four breeding pairs to 10 ha in good habitat, and there is over 200 sq km of pure Corsican Pine woodland on Corsica. The species will also nest in less suitable habitats, including mixed woodland, though breeding densities are much lower here.

Generally speaking, the birds are resident in the high pine forests, though young or unmated birds may move lower in winter into pine plantations, chestnut or beech woodland, or even gardens. The mature paired birds stay high, though there may be some vertical movement in bad weather, especially after heavy snow. It is very difficult to estimate the total Corsican population – in other words, the world population – in the spectacular and inaccessible mountain ranges that form the bird's prime habitat, but the best current estimates suggest between 3,000 and 9,000 individual birds. This is not a large population, but it seems to be more or less stable, and not under any great threat, especially as much of its habitat lies within the semi-protected Corsican Natural Regional Park. The best places to see the Corsican Nuthatch are in the higher parts of the Asco Valley and the Verghello Valley.

Since 2002, the distinctive Corsican race or subspecies of the Citril Finch (*Carduelis citrinella*) has been separated as a new species, the Corsican Finch (*C. corsicanus*). This bird differs from the Citril Finch in having darker brown streaked upper parts and brighter yellow underparts, as well as different habits and a slightly different call. It is not a strict Corsican endemic, as it also occurs on Sardinia and a number of other Italian islands. Interestingly, the Citril Finch is almost always a high-altitude bird on the mainland, but its Corsican relative is much more widespread and catholic in its tastes, filling a wide range of ecological niches.

Wetland Birds

As already noted, France is particularly rich in wetlands of many sorts, including coastal wetlands that lie below high-tide levels. It comes as little surprise, therefore, that it is exceptionally rich in water birds of all sorts. It is estimated that around 160 wetland sites in France are important enough to qualify as Important Bird Areas (IBAs) for their populations of wetland birds. These IBAs are sites of European importance, assessed on various criteria, such as the percentage of the total world population of a species that breeds on or uses a site, and the total number of species present.

Breeding wetland birds with good numbers in France include the Great Crested and Black-necked Grebes ((*Podiceps cristatus* and *P. nigricollis*), Bittern (*Botaurus stellaris*) and Little Bittern (*Ixobrychus minutus*), all the other regular European herons (see Camargue, page 105), many of the more widespread ducks and also rarer species such as the Red-crested Pochard (*Netta rufina*), and three species of crake – Baillon's Crake (*Porzana pusilla*), the Little Crake (*P. parva*) and the Spotted Crake (*P. porzana*) – though finding any of these last three is another matter. Kingfishers (*Alcedo atthis*) are common everywhere at all times of the year, though there is a good deal of migration around the country according to weather conditions. There are also plenty of wetland warblers such as Savi's Warbler (*Locustella*

ABOVE, LEFT A Kingfisher bringing its catch to a perch near the nest.

ABOVE, CENTRE Savi's Warblers have been spreading northwards in France in recent years.

ABOVE, RIGHT Great Reed Warblers are the most visible of the reed warblers, singing openly from the tops of reeds.

BELOW The beautiful Red-crested Pochard is relatively common on the wetlands of southern France.

ABOVE Young White Storks practising their flying skills before leaving the nest, which was built on a house rooftop.

luscinioides), the Grasshopper Warbler (*L. naevia*), Cetti's Warbler (*Cettia cetti*), which has extended its range northwards in recent years, the Great Reed Warbler (*Acrocephalus arundinaceus*), Marsh Warbler (*A. palustris*) and more widespread species such as the Sedge Warbler (*A. schoenobaenus*).

The White Stork (*Ciconia ciconia*) is an iconic bird that is widespread in much of eastern and northern Europe as a breeding species, though it has generally declined in the western part of its range. In France, however, aided by some reintroduction, it has begun to increase again as a breeding bird, and there are now quite strong populations in south-west France around Arcachon, in Normandy and in Alsace; the number of breeding pairs rose from 315 in 1995 to 641 in 2000. The Parc Ornithologique at Teich, on the Bassin d'Arcachon – much more of a nature reserve than a park – has a strong and readily visible population, and there is a good rehabilitation and reintroduction centre at Hunawihr, north-west of Colmar in Alsace. White Storks also migrate through France in quite large numbers and are increasingly wintering

in southern France – for example, numbers rose from 8 in 1996–7 to 172 in 2003–4.

The Lac du Der-Chantecocq Story

In the low-lying 'Wet Champagne' country south-west of St Dizier lies one of the largest lakes in France. It has only been in existence since 1974, yet it has already become a wonderful and important site for birds and other aspects of nature.

The lake was created as part of a plan to reduce flooding on the Seine and Marne Rivers and, when full, covers an area of 48 sq km. Unlike most reservoirs, which are in steep-sided valleys to maximize the effects of the dam, the Lac du Der is in quite level countryside. This means that when the water levels rise and fall, they expose or flood huge areas of mud and marshland rather than bare, sterile, stony valley sides.

As a result, in just over 30 years the lake has become a hugely productive wetland ecosystem, with an enormous range of species resident, breeding or just visiting. It is designated as an internationally important wetland under the Ramsar Convention, and as an EU Important Bird Area, and is now managed as a very large nature reserve by the French national hunting department (ONCFS). The birds recorded here amount to 270 species, and there are also 50 species of dragonfly and damselfly (including rarities like the Orange-spotted Emerald), 40 species of mammal, 20 amphibians and hundreds of plants. In the breeding season there are Savi's Warblers, Little Bitterns (and possibly Bitterns, though these may no longer breed), Purple Herons (*Ardea purpurea*), here towards the northern edge of their breeding range, Little Egrets (*Egretta garzetta*), Night Herons (*Nycticorax nycticorax*) and Great Crested Grebes, among others. Other likely birds appear to be testing the water: for example, Great White Egrets (*Ardea alba*) are now resident all year round in quite good numbers, and mating has been seen, though no nests or young have yet been discovered, and Black-necked Grebes are increasingly staying through the breeding season.

It is, however, as a passage and wintering site that the lake has become best known, and especially for its extraordinary populations of Common Cranes (*Grus grus*). These breed in northern Europe and Russia, then migrate southwards or south-westwards to wintering grounds in Spain and Africa. The Lac du Der is roughly on their pre-existing route, and they quickly discovered it as a useful staging post. However, its importance to the birds has steadily increased, and they are staying longer and longer. Generally speaking, peak numbers are reached in October–November (76,000 birds were recorded in November 2000, for example) with a smaller peak in spring (up to about 35,000 birds) as the migration route is slightly further east on the northwards journey. Increasingly, though, birds are staying on here through the winter – for example, on 10 January 2008, there were 10,500 around the lake. This may be partly a behavioural trend, but it also depends on the severity of the winters (which are very mild at the time of writing), and few birds are likely to stay if the winter is harsh. In the last 20 years or so, the lake has become the single most important stopover for the European population of Common Cranes; almost half of the estimated population of nearly a quarter of a million birds stops over here at some point, enjoying the lack of disturbance at their roosts and the rich feeding in the fields around the lake.

Other wintering birds here include Bewick's and Whooper Swans (*Cygnus columbianus* and *C. cygnus*), the Bean Goose (*Anser fabalis*), White-fronted Goose (*A. albifrons*), Smew (*Mergellus albellus*), Goosander (*Mergus merganser*), Red-breasted Merganser (*M. serrator*) and many others. The site has also become famous for its White-tailed Eagles (*Haliaeetus albicilla*), but there are never more than a very few birds, and in some recent years they have not been seen at all.

Altogether, it is an extraordinary site, and one that gives hope for the possibilities of creation of other good sites to replace some of the many wetlands lost over the last 50 years.

TOP, RIGHT A Night Heron in its nesting tree close to the Lac du Der.
CENTRE, RIGHT Red-breasted Mergansers regularly winter at Chantecocq and elsewhere in France.
BOTTOM, RIGHT Whooper Swans breed in the Arctic, but pass the winter on lakes in Europe.

Coastal Birds

France has an enormous length of coastline, along the English Channel, Atlantic Ocean and Mediterranean Sea, with a superb variety of habitats in different climatic zones. It also has a fine variety of breeding seabirds – about 30 species – though for once its central position in Europe works against it to a degree. If you took away the seabird populations of the two extremes of Corsica and western Brittany, France's seabird tally would be rather poor, as most seabirds tend to be strongly northern, feeding on the rich resources of the north Atlantic, or southern, and there are rather fewer in the middle.

Northern Group

The northern group is the largest, and France is on the southern limit of the range of most of these birds; the majority nest only on the northern and north-western coasts, and are often confined to just a few sites in Brittany, the most oceanic part of France. The Fulmar (*Fulmarus glacialis*) resembles a gull in some ways, but is actually in the shearwater family Procellariidae, close to the albatrosses. It spread southwards in the middle part of the 20th century, first being confirmed as a breeding bird in France in 1960 on the Sept-Iles (home of France's major seabird colonies), and continuing to increase in numbers through the 1970s, though population numbers have

ABOVE A pair of Fulmars at its nest; these birds have increased markedly in northern France over recent decades.

BELOW Gannets breed in France as a single vast colony in Brittany numbering about 17,000 pairs.

now stabilized at a little over a thousand pairs. The related Manx Shearwater (*Puffinus puffinus*) – known in France as the 'Puffin des Anglais', though it is not related to the Puffin (*Fraterculus arcticus*) – has a similar distribution, with about 200 pairs currently nesting on the islands. Like a number of other seabirds, the Manx Shearwater nests in burrows and is drastically affected by the presence of any rats, which is why it tends to breed on offshore islands. At present, serious efforts are being made to rid several islands of invasive rats in the hope of increasing numbers of this and other species. The European Storm Petrel (*Hydrobates pelagicus*) follows a similar distribution pattern, though it does also have some very small colonies in southern France.

Gannets (*Morus bassanus*) first reached France as breeding birds in about 1939, on Sept-Iles again (Ile Rouzic), and since then the single colony has grown to about 17,000 pairs – an extraordinary rate of expansion fuelled by overflow from the burgeoning British colonies. Gannets are wide-ranging, powerful fliers, generally moving southwards into African waters in winter, so colonization of new sites – if conditions are right – is relatively easy. A visit to a Gannet colony in early summer is a wonderful experience, with thousands of the beautiful white birds flying to and fro, and often plunge-diving close to the shore. Access onto Ile Rouzic is restricted, but excellent views of the Gannets – and many other birds – can be had from regular boat trips.

The Atlantic form of the Shag (*Phalacrocorax aristotelis aristotelis*) has followed a rather similar pattern, increasing from

just a few pairs at the start of the 20th century to about 6,000 pairs today, mainly spread around the coast of Brittany, where they can be seen regularly all year round. The Lesser Black-backed Gull (*Larus fuscus*) – a European endemic – has also increased dramatically, from about 1,000 pairs in 1955 up to almost 23,000 pairs now, which is about 8 per cent of the world population. The gulls are common along most of the Channel and Brittany coasts, mixing with Herring Gulls (*L.*

ABOVE A Kittiwake at its nest on a cliff ledge with two young; these birds are now a common sight in Brittany.
ABOVE, RIGHT Common Terns now breed widely in France, both on coastal sites and along the major rivers.
BELOW With their striking multicoloured beaks, Puffins are the most distinctive of the auks, though they are now rare breeding birds in France.

argentatus), which were also rare a hundred years ago but are now abundant, and Great Black-backed Gulls (*L. marinus*) – unknown in France until the 1920s but now quite common. Kittiwakes (*Rissa tridactyla*) are lovely, delicate gulls that spend most of their time far out on the oceans, coming ashore only to breed. Like most of the other seabirds so far described, they increased markedly in the second half of the 20th century, reaching roughly stable numbers now of around 6,000 pairs,

mainly on the cliffs of Brittany and Normandy. The coastal terns (*Sterna* spp.) are a distinctive group of elegant seabirds, which are almost like large swallows in flight, fishing by making steep dives from quite a height. In France, they are not particularly northern or coastal as a group, and the only species confined to the north is the rare Roseate Tern (*S. dougallii*), which has one major colony of around 100 pairs, down from about 500 pairs in 1973.

The colonies tend to move quite frequently, probably to try to reduce predation by local ground predators such as the Red Fox (*Vulpes vulpes*), which can quickly decimate an accessible colony once it has been discovered, though with these species the general decline of most northern populations may also be partly caused by trapping in their African wintering areas. The Common Tern (*Sterna hirundo*) has a number of coastal breeding sites in France, but in recent years it has become more frequent on inland waters, especially up the Loire River.

The auk family, Alcidae, comprises only oceanic birds, with six European species that are all strongly northern in their distribution. France just extends into the southernmost edge of this range, and has three breeding species, all with a tenuous foothold and all confined to Brittany. The most endangered of these is the Razorbill (*Alca torda*), which is considered to be the rarest of French seabirds and one of the rarest of all French birds; at present there are only about 23 pairs in one colony, with very small numbers elsewhere. Although the Razorbill has declined generally, there are still very large populations further north in Europe, so it is not globally threatened. The rather similar Common Guillemot (*Uria*

aalge) is faring slightly better, with about 250 pairs, all in Brittany, and mostly on the cliffs of Cap Fréhel, west of St Malo. Finally, the Puffin, the most distinctive of the auks, with its wonderful, huge, multicoloured beak and comical habits, has declined severely in France, in common with other southern outposts of the main population, and there are only 200 or so pairs, mostly on the Sept-Iles.

A Visit to Les Sept-Iles

The little group of islands known as Sept-Iles (because there are, roughly, seven islands) lies just off the north Brittany coast near Perros-Guirec, north-east of Morlaix. The islands hold the most important seabird colonies in France, with a marvellous selection of birds, as listed below. They are managed as one of the National Nature Reserve series by the LPO, who have an excellent Visitor Centre on the nearby Ile Grande (accessible by road) – phone 0296919140 or email ile-grande@lpo.fr

Species	Approximate number of breeding pairs
Gannet	17,000+
Herring Gull	2,700
Great Black-backed Gull	80
Lesser Black-backed Gull	650
Manx Shearwater	150
Fulmar	80
European Storm Petrel	45
Shag	350
Common Tern	5
Common Guillemot	12
Razorbill	23
Puffin	160

The islands also support breeding Ravens (*Corvus corax*), Oystercatchers (*Haematopus ostralegus*), Grey Seals

ABOVE, LEFT Guillemots breed in small numbers on the cliffs of Brittany, and often gather just offshore in the breeding season.
ABOVE, RIGHT The Oystercatcher breeds regularly on Sept-Iles and elsewhere along the Brittany coast.
BELOW Razorbills are currently extremely rare breeding birds in France, with just a handful of pairs breeding on the north-west coast.

ABOVE A Sandwich Tern bringing food to its nest in the Camargue.
BELOW Little Terns breed mainly on sandy beaches, where they are very
subject to disturbance by humans using the same habitat.

(*Halichoerus grypus*) and many other species of interest. With
a few exceptions, there is no landing, but excellent boat trips,
often with an LPO guide, can be made from the harbour at
Trestraou (Perros-Guirec) from April to June for about 15 euros.
These give good views of almost all the birds either fishing or
roosting at sea, or around the breeding grounds.

Southern Group

The southern group of seabirds is rather smaller, and perhaps
less well known. Cory's Shearwater (*Calonectris diomedea*) is a
surprisingly large bird, with a wingspan of
over a metre. It breeds around the coast of
Corsica and on a few islands off the south-
east part of the mainland, and has a total
population of 1,000–1,300 pairs. All the
birds in France are the Mediterranean subspecies (ssp. *diomedea*). The closely related
Yelkouan Shearwater (*Puffinus yelkouan*),
previously treated as a race of the Manx
Shearwater, is rather smaller (wingspan up to
about 80 cm) and darker. It is a rare bird in
France, with just a few hundred pairs breeding mainly on the Iles d'Hyères off the
Provence coast near Toulon.

The Shag also has a separate
Mediterranean subspecies (*Phalacrocorax
aristotelis desmarestii*), quite distinct in range
from the more northerly subspecies and with
much whiter young birds. In France, it is almost confined as a
breeding species to Corsica, where about 90 per cent of the
French population occurs in a series of west coast cliff sites.
There are also a number of gulls that have their main or entire
range in the Mediterranean Sea. The least common gull in
France is Audouin's Gull (*Larus audouinii*) – a Mediterranean
endemic – which is an attractive slender, pale gull, with a deep
red beak. Within France, this species only breeds on Corsica,
with a total population of about 60–100 pairs scattered around
the island and not doing very well, though it is surprising how
often you see them.

The Mediterranean Gull (*L. melanocephalus*) was a rare bird
in France until the 1950s, but since then it has gradually
expanded its range. Its principle stronghold is still the
Camargue, though there are now many
other small colonies virtually throughout the
country. It resembles the more widespread
Black-headed Gull (*L. ridibundus*), but has a
blacker head, heavier bill and wings that are
very white underneath. The Slender-billed
Gull (*L. genei*) used to be a quite rare eastern
and southern species, but has expanded its
range and numbers. France still only has a
rather small population of 600–800 pairs,
wholly confined to a couple of lagoons in
the Camargue. It is a distinctive bird, with –
appropriately enough – a very slender red
bill, and there is a distinct pinkish tinge to
the underparts in birds with fresh plumage.

The remaining gull with a Mediterranean
distribution in France is the Yellow-Legged
Gull (*L. michahellis*) – essentially the southern version of the Herring Gull, with similar
appearance and habits except for the yellow
legs. It has increased enormously in south-

ern France in recent decades, and there are now over 40,000 pairs, mainly in the south though the birds are steadily spreading northwards.

Finally, there are a few terns that are primarily southern in France. The key species here is the Gull-billed Tern (*Gelochelidon nilotica*), an almost worldwide species in the tropics and southern temperate zones that just reaches into southern France. Here, as a breeding species, it is confined to the saltpans or lagoons of the Camargue, with a population of 300–400 pairs. At the moment, it seems unable to expand because of competition from the burgeoning Yellow-legged Gull populations, though some culling of the latter takes place. It is a large tern, with a heavy black bill and longer legs than other terns, almost intermediate in appearance between gulls and terns. Two other terns occur more commonly in the Mediterranean area than elsewhere – the Sandwich Tern (*Sterna sandvicensis*) and Little Tern (*S. albifrons*) – though neither is a specifically southern species. Good numbers of Sandwich Terns also winter in France, though they are probably birds from the Black Sea or further north rather than French breeding birds.

Bird Life in the Camargue

The Camargue is an extraordinary area, almost certainly the best year-round birdwatching site in France, yet also full of other treasures from Stripeless Tree Frogs (*Hyla meridionalis*) to orchids. It is a wetland area that is situated around the point where the various arms of the River Rhône meet the Mediterranean Sea, forming a vast and varied delta made up of lagoons, salt marshes, sand dunes, reed beds, woodland and other habitats. Most of the area that has not been drained or converted into rice paddies now lies within the Parc Naturel Régional de Camargue, which covers about 850 sq km between the City of Arles and the coast at Stes Mairies de la Mer. In spring and early summer, the area is alive with birds, here to breed and raise their young.

Some of the special breeding birds, in addition to the coastal birds mentioned above, include several hundred Red-crested Pochards (*Netta rufina*), dozens of Marsh Harriers (*Circus aeruginosus*), beautiful Black-winged Stilts (*Himantopus himantopus*) on almost every little lagoon, and Avocets (*Recurvirostra avosetta*) and Kentish Plovers (*Charadrius alexandrinus*) all along the coastline. This is a particularly good area for the heron family, with all the French species to be found here, often in large numbers. Both Grey and Purple Herons (*Ardea cinerea* and *A. purpurea*) are common – the former a recent arrival – and there are some fine (though generally inaccessible) mixed breeding colonies of the

ABOVE, RIGHT Yellow-legged Gulls, essentially the southern counterpart of the Herring Gull, are now very common in southern France.

BELOW, RIGHT The elegant Black-winged Stilt breeds around lagoons and pools throughout the Camargue area.

ABOVE A pair of Greater Flamingoes in flight. These birds are now the icon of the Camargue, commonly seen all year round.

LEFT The Purple Heron is just one of the heron family that is doing well on the extraordinary wetland area of the Camargue.

Squacco Heron (*Ardeola ralloides*), Night Heron, Little Egret and Cattle Egret (*Bubulcus ibis*). The Cattle Egret was unknown here until 1968 – now there are more than 1,000 pairs, and they are spreading throughout France and beyond. Spoonbills (*Platalea leucorodia*) now breed in small numbers, and Great White Egrets have started staying all year round.

The undoubted star among the breeding birds is the Greater Flamingo, of which there are about 15,000 pairs as well as many non-breeding birds. Numbers vary, as flamingoes are very mobile and will simply move south to the warmer Spanish breeding site if the Camargue gets too cold, or return if Spain is too dry. Not surprisingly given these numbers, they can be seen almost everywhere in the Camargue, and are often quite approachable.

Apart from these essentially wetland species, there are a number of other interesting birds that breed here, using different aspects of the Camargue's wild habitats. They include the Hoopoe (*Upupa epops*), European Bee-eater (*Merops apiaster*), Great Spotted Cuckoo (*Clamator glandularius*), which mainly parasitizes Magpies (*Pica pica*) and other members of the crow family, European Roller (*Coracias garrulus*), Tawny

Pipit (*Anthus campestris*) and Woodchat Shrike (*Lanius senator*), to name but a few.

Spring and early summer are probably the best times to visit the Camargue, but winter is good for birds, too. The flamingoes, some of the herons and some other birds are resident, with their numbers swelled by huge numbers of wintering birds, especially waterfowl such as the Mallard (*Anas platyrhynchos*), up to 30,000 birds; Teal (*A. crecca*), up to 25,000; Wigeon (*A. penelope*), up to 15,000; Gadwall (*A. strepera*), up to 13,000, and many others. Most waders pass through in spring and autumn, but others, such as the Golden Plover (*Pluvialis apricaria*), tend to stay on. All these birds attract predators, of course, and it is not uncommon to see one or two Spotted Eagles (*Aquila clanga*) or White-tailed Eagles, as well as the more common Peregrine Falcons (*Falco peregrinus*) and other birds of prey.

Migrating Birds

France straddles several major flyways for migrating birds, and every year many millions of birds migrate into, out of and through the country. There are several categories of migrant bird. Firstly, there are those that arrive from warmer southern climates to spend the summer in France nesting and rearing young, including vast numbers of insectivorous warblers and flycatchers, specialist birds of prey such as the Short-toed Eagle (*Circaetus gallicus*), which feeds mainly on snakes, and many others. These all leave in winter because there is not enough food for them.

Another group of birds is the passage migrants – those that pass through France in spring and autumn on their way to and from different destinations, but not stopping to breed in France. This group includes the Common Crane and many Arctic-breeding waders. A third category of birds spend just the winter in France, breeding elsewhere – usually further north – but finding plenty of food in France to carry them through. These are mostly waders and water birds. In addition, there are birds that just move locally within the region, and there are many birds that do more than one of the above.

For the observer, it is a wonderful experience to be present when some of these mass movements of birds are taking place, and fortunately birds are fairly predictable in their habits. In general, they try to avoid high-altitude mountain crossings and long water crossings, so there are many bottlenecks such as low cols in high mountain ranges, deep north–south oriented valleys, and headlands projecting far out into the water that are

TOP, RIGHT A dazzlingly beautiful European Bee-eater at its nest site in an earth bank in southern France.
CENTRE, RIGHT Hoopoes are exotic-looking birds, most often seen feeding on the ground or flying their slow, butterfly-like flight.
BOTTOM, RIGHT Rollers are rare summer visitors to southern France, nesting in just a few favoured locations such as the Camargue.

ABOVE A group of Griffon Vultures near Troumouse. Vultures are
increasing in France from sites in the Pyrenees and the Massif Central.

inevitably likely to attract the highest numbers of birds. Many
smaller birds migrate in relatively straight lines because they
are less affected by considerations such as water crossings than
larger birds, and they may also migrate at night, so they are
harder to watch.

Larger birds such as storks, eagles, buzzards and kites need
to adopt a different strategy from that of the smaller birds.
Because of their weight, they are strongly reliant on using thermals rising from warmed ground to gain altitude so that they
can glide for long distances in their chosen direction. There are
no significant thermals over water, so their whole migration
strategy in Europe involves taking the shortest crossings across
the Mediterranean. Thus, large numbers fly south-westwards in
autumn, to cross the Mediterranean around the Straits of
Gibraltar, while others move down Italy and on to Sicily, or
eastwards to fly round the eastern end of the Mediterranean,
with major bottlenecks at the Bosphorus and in Israel. It is the
south-westerly flying birds (and their spring counterparts) that
pass through France, and almost inevitably this means that
they need to pass through the Pyrenees, the Massif Central and
one or other of the eastern mountains.

As a result, there are some excellent migration-watching
points in these mountains, many of which have regular seasonal information points manned by the LPO and others. One
of the best is the Col d'Organbidexka in the western Pyrenees,
near Larrau. At its best, this is one of the best migration points
in Western Europe, with many thousands of birds per season,
including up to 20 species of birds of prey. As many as 18,000
Honey Buzzards (*Pernis apivorus*) and 13,000 Black Kites
(*Milvus migrans*) may pass through, as well as both White and
Black Storks (*Ciconia ciconia* and *C. nigra*), Common Cranes,
Woodpigeons (*Columba palumbus*), various thrushes and
other species.

Peak bird migration numbers are from late August to late
October. Unfortunately, there are people whose aim is not to
watch and enjoy the birds, but to shoot them, and this col has
long been an area of controversy between hunters and conservationists. Fortunately, those wanting to protect the birds have
the upper hand at present, though there is still a line of shooting hides on the col.

Further east in the Pyrenees, around the village of Eyne (just
south-east of Font Romeu), there is another excellent area,
dominated mainly by birds of prey (especially Honey
Buzzards), storks and bee-eaters.

In the Massif Central, the Col de Prat de Bouc, lying at
about 1,500 m near the Plomb du Cantal, is a superb area,

ABOVE Common Cranes pass through France on migration, and more and more are staying on through the winter, often feeding on agricultural land. RIGHT The Common Buzzard is a stocky raptor that lives in all kinds of forest and mountains, and marshy and rocky coasts, but always close to open areas. Northern European birds migrate to France in the winter.

with 300,000–400,000 birds regularly counted in autumn, including Black Kites (*Milvus migrans*), Honey Buzzards and Ring Ouzels (*Turdus torquatus*). Another good place in the Auvergne is the Montagne de la Serre, south of Clermont-Ferrand, where over the period between 1986 and 2004, 176 species were recorded, with 70 regulars including Common Cranes, Common Buzzards (*Buteo buteo*), Honey Buzzards and Red Kites (*Milvus milvus*).

Most of these sites are at their best in autumn, but there are others such as Cap Leucate on the Mediterranean coast, north of Perpignan, which are at their best in spring, with northward-moving migrants. Here, birds that are having difficulty crossing the Pyrenees may be pushed eastwards, especially if there is a wind from the north-west, and end up gathering around Leucate. This site is best between mid-February and May. There are other excellent sites in Provence, the Jura, the Vosges and elsewhere, many of them listed on the LPO's website, www.lpo.fr.

Chapter 6
THE MAMMALS OF FRANCE

There are about 135 species of mammal in France, depending on how many of the marine mammals are included, and which of the introduced species are considered to be worth including. None of these mammals is endemic solely to France, though a few, such as the Pyrenean Desman (see page 114), are endemic to France and adjacent areas only.

LEFT A herd of wild Ibex in the high Alps along the Italian border.

ONE SPECIES OF MAMMAL OCCURRING IN FRANCE, the Mediterranean Monk Seal (*Monachus monachus*), is classified as Critically Endangered in the International Union for the Conservation of Nature's (IUCN's) Red List of Threatened Animals (although perhaps it should be provisionally considered extinct until populations in the eastern Mediterranean grow enough for it to recolonize French sites). Two species – the European Mink (*Mustela lutreola*) and Northern Right Whale (*Eubalaena glacialis*) – are rated as Endangered. Many more are classified as Vulnerable, among them several bats (see below).

Bats

There are 29 species of bat recorded in France, amounting to about a fifth of the mammal fauna, yet they are rather little known by the layperson. Most people have noticed bats flying at dusk, especially in the southern parts of France, but few know much about their identification, habits and distribution. The advent of relatively inexpensive bat detectors (hand-held devices that amplify the sounds made by bats to make them audible to the human ear) has revolutionized their study in recent years, and a realization that many species have declined

BELOW A Lesser Horseshoe Bat hanging in characteristic fashion from the roof of a cave.

dramatically has given an impetus to more detailed research and census work. With the aid of such a detector and suitable information, it is now possible to identify most species of bat, though there are still limitations, especially on deep-forest species and others that call very little. The bats of France fall into three distinct families.

Horseshoe Bats

The horseshoe bats, Rhinolophidae, are very distinctive, and all have a curious horseshoe-shaped fleshy structure around the nostrils, through which the echolocation signals are emitted while the mouth remains shut. Perhaps more obvious is their habit of hanging freely by their toes, so they are readily visible if found in a roost or hibernation site. There are four species of this family in France: the Greater Horsehoe Bat (*Rhinolophus ferrumequinum*), Lesser Horseshoe Bat (*R. hipposideros*), Mediterranean Horseshoe Bat (*R. euryale*) and Mehely's Horseshoe Bat (*R. mehelyi*).

The Greater Horseshoe Bat is an impressive creature with a wingspan of 30–35 cm. It is a social animal, often occurring in large colonies in caves and buildings, though it is rarely seen without prior knowledge, as individuals do not usually emerge until nearly an hour after sunset. If you do get the chance to watch a roost, the emergence can be spectacular as hundreds of large bats pour out from the exit just before the last light disappears. The Mediterranean Horseshoe Bat is much more restricted in range, confined to the warmer parts of France, though the rarest is probably Mehely's Horseshoe Bat, which is classed as Vulnerable, though it is almost certainly still underrecorded due to confusion with the other species.

Vespertilionidae

The great majority of French bats belong to the family Vespertilionidae. These bats do not have the horseshoe structure, echolocate through their open mouths, and generally roost and hibernate in crevices, though a few will hang freely. This family includes the pipistrelles, mouse-eared bats, noctules, Daubenton's Bat (*Myotis daubentonii*) and the long-eared bats.

Daubenton's Bat and its similar close relatives, the Nathalina Bat (*M. nathalinae*), Long-fingered Bat (*M. capaccinii*) and Pond Bat (*M. dasycneme*), are attractive bats, quite frequently seen because of their predictable habits of hunting low over water bodies such as rivers and ponds. All are of medium size and brownish, with a wingspan of about 25 cm; Daubenton's occurs throughout France, the Long-fingered is a Mediterranean coastal species, while the Pond Bat is an eastern species that just reaches into north-eastern France. The Nathalina Bat is still relatively under-recorded, as it was only separated in 1977 from the morphologically very similar Daubenton's Bat – in fact, many zoologists feel that the split is not a valid one. It is always worth scanning well-vegetated ponds and rivers after dusk in spring and summer to see if any

BATS OF THE RHONE-ALPES

To give a better idea of the richness of the French bat fauna, it is interesting to see the range of species recorded in one region of France – Rhône-Alpes, made up of eight departments, mainly in the Alps. About 27 species of bat have been recorded here (though some occurred only sporadically, or are possibly now extinct):

Bechstein's Bat (*Myotis bechsteinii*) Widespread but probably rare.
Lesser Mouse-eared Bat (*M. blythii*) Locally common in summer only.
Brandt's Bat (*M. brandti*) Very rare and local.
Long-fingered Bat (*M. capaccinii*) Very local, in Ardèche only, at northern edge of its range.
Daubenton's Bat (*M. daubentonii*) Widespread and common.
Geoffroy's Bat (*M. emarginatus*) Widespread though uncommon.
Greater Mouse-eared Bat (*M. myotis*) Widespread and moderately common.
Whiskered Bat (*M. mystacinus*) Widespread and moderately common in breeding season.
Natterer's Bat (*M. nattereri*) Widespread and common throughout.
Barbastelle (*Barbastella barbastellus*) Widespread and moderately common.
Northern Bat (*Eptesicus nilssoni*) Uncommon; mainly in alpine areas, close to southern edge of its range.
Serotine (*E. serotinus*) Widespread and common.
Savi's Pipistrelle (*Hypsugo*, or *Pipistrellus*, *savii*) Quite

ABOVE A Noctule Bat, one of the larger species of bat, hanging on the bark of a tree.

common in southern part of region; at northern edge of its French range.
Greater Noctule (*Nyctalus lasiopterus*) Extremely rare; old records only.
Leisler's Bat (*N. leisleri*) Quite common; a notoriously hard bat to census due to its woodland habitat.
Noctule (*N. noctula*) Widespread and moderately common.
Kuhl's Pipistrelle (*Pipistrellus kuhlii*) Common, especially in warmer lowland areas.
Nathusius' Pipistrelle (*P. nathusii*) Widespread but local.
Common Pipistrelle (*P. pipistrellus*) Widespread and common up to high altitudes in the Alps.
Brown Long-eared Bat (*Plecotus auritus*) Widespread and common.
Grey Long-eared Bat (*P. austriacus*) Widespread and common.
Parti-coloured Bat (*Vespertilio murinus*) Rare; confined to mountain areas, where it is at western edge of its range.
Schreiber's Bat (*Miniopterus schreibersii*) Widespread and locally common.
European Free-tailed Bat (*Tadarida teniotis*) Surprisingly frequent and widespread, with noticeable recent increase in records due to use of bat detectors.
Mediterranean Horseshoe Bat (*Rhinolopus euryale*) Uncommon or rare; mainly in Ardèche.
Greater Horseshoe Bat (*R. ferrumequinum*) Widespread and common.
Lesser Horseshoe Bat (*R. hipposideros*) Widespread and common.

---

of these species are about – on a good stretch of water they can occur in large numbers. They constantly hunt low over the water, when they are a spectacular sight.

Noctule Bats
Three very large bats occur in France, all with wingspans of almost half a metre, though they are all still remarkably light in weight, rarely weighing more than 50g. The largest of these bats, in body weight at least, is the Greater Noctule (*Nyctalus lasiopterus*), which is similar to but distinctly larger than the more familiar Noctule (*N. noctula*).

The Greater Noctule is a rare species apparently found only in the south-western coastal regions and occasionally in the Alps. In 2001, evidence came to light that rocked the zoological world – feathers of migrant species of bird were found in the droppings of this species, leading to the suggestion that these bats preyed on birds. Recent work has demonstrated that they do indeed feed on birds; it would appear that they catch

ABOVE The Pyrenean Desman is a highly specialized aquatic insectivore that forages for crustaceans and insect larvae mainly at night.

A Pyrenean Oddity: the Pyrenean Desman

The Pyrenean Desman (*Galemys pyrenaicus*) is a fascinating little animal, though seldom seen because of its nocturnal and aquatic habits, and its comparative rarity. It is a relative of the moles, and resembles an aquatic mole more than anything – brown, about 10–15 cm long, with a tail as long again and a very long, narrow, flexible snout.

Desmans have very poor vision, and their snouts act as the main sensory organ for detecting food, members of the opposite sex and danger. Their main habitat is the cold rivers of the middle to higher altitude Pyrenees, up to about 2,000 m, where they feed almost exclusively on insects and invertebrates. They may be active in the day for a short period, but it seems that they are much less likely to be predated by Eurasian Otters (*Lutra lutra*), White Storks and other diurnal predators if they are active mainly at night.

There is a small population in France that appears to be developing a different way of life – this is confined to a group of high lakes in the Ayou area, which are frozen almost solidly for about six months of the year. The population of desmans here seems to take to subterranean rivers for the winter, and may eventually become troglodytes! There is no accurate estimate of the French population of desmans, but one estimate, based on extrapolating from known populations and an assessment of the habitat available, suggests that there may be as many as 17,000 individuals.

migrating passerine birds on the wing at night at altitudes of 1,000 m or more. Each year, approximately five billion passerines cross the Mediterranean basin during their autumn migrations, and yet virtually nothing preys on those moving at night. This new work shows that Greater Noctules prey heavily on migrant birds in spring and especially autumn, and that they probably time their breeding seasons to coincide with maximum prey availability, rather like the diurnal avian predator Eleonora's Falcon (*Falco eleonorae*) – a Mediterranean species found occasionally in France. Little is known of the predation mechanism, but the bats are assumed to both catch and eat the birds on the wing, discarding the less edible parts as they fly.

The Greater Mouse-eared Bat (*Myotis myotis*) is almost as large as the Greater Noctule, though it is rather lighter in weight, brown above and pale greyish-white below. These bats usually hang free in roosts, and have been likened to hanging rabbits! They prey on various large insects caught both on the wing and from the ground, and may even land and search on the ground for crickets and other nocturnal insects.

Free-tailed Bats

The third very large bat is the only European member of a different family, the Molossidae. This is the European Free-tailed Bat (*Tadarida teniotis*), so-called because the tail (normally invisible in other species as it is part of the rear flight membrane) projects well beyond the membrane and is visible in flight. This bat is very large, with short, fine, dark greyish fur, long, broad ears, a distinctive straight, fast flight and an unmistakeable silhouette. It is mainly a species of southern mountain areas, along the Mediterranean coast and up into the Maritime Alps as high as 2,000 m or so. It particularly likes limestone areas with caves, gorges and crevices, where it roosts, emerging at night to feed on insects (and who knows what else?).

Carnivores

Grey Wolf

The Grey Wolf (*Canis lupus*) has a tenuous foothold in France. It became extinct during the 1930s, with the last known animal killed in Limousin in 1937, but it is beginning to edge back into the French Alps from the mobile population in northern Italy. This population occupies an area that includes most of the western Alps in France and Italy, with the majority of the pack territories being cross-boundary along the French–Italian border south of Valle d'Aosta. Perhaps unsurprisingly, its increasing presence here is controversial, especially where it comes into contact with the sheep-herders.

Brown Bear

The presence of Brown Bears (*Ursus arctos*) in France is an even more controversial and politically sensitive issue. They

OPPOSITE, TOP The Grey Wolf is slowly increasing in numbers in alpine France, despite opposition to its presence from farmers and others.
OPPOSITE, BELOW The magnificent Brown Bear is once again to be seen in remote areas of the Pyrenees due to the introduction of bears from Slovakia.

ABOVE A Common Weasel, the smallest of the weasel family to be found in France, hunting during the day.
BELOW The strikingly marked Western Polecat, with its distinctive facial mask, is widespread throughout the wooded parts of France.

probably became extinct, or effectively extinct, as a natural population in France in the 1970s, but since then a series of reintroductions of Slovakian bears into the Pyrenees has taken place, provoking strong adverse reactions from local farmers and hunters, and equally strong positive responses from naturalists, conservationists and others. A series of 'accidents' has befallen the introduced bears: one, which happened to be the last female in France, was shot in 'self-defence' by a group of hunters in 2004, another was killed in a road accident and yet another died in a cliff fall. At the time of the first of these incidents, President Jacques Chirac said: 'The disappearance of a species is always a serious loss for biodiversity,' and the environment minister Serge Lepeltier said: 'It is an ecological catastrophe because this was the last female bear of the Pyrenean line,' which appears to indicate that there is a strong political will behind the reintroductions.

Despite the setbacks, the reintroduction programme is continuing with the aim of bringing the bear population up to self-sustaining numbers in several locations along the Pyrenees. The bears mainly live in the higher forested areas at about 1,300–2,000 m, ranging over very large territories; the territories of some males, for instance, may be as large as 1,000 sq km.

The Weasel Family

There are a number of members of the weasel family, the Mustelidae, in France. The introduced American Mink (*Mustela vison*) is becoming more common, but much less well known is the endangered European Mink (*M. lutreola*). It is rather similar to the American Mink in appearance, though generally more shy and nocturnal, and with a distinctly white chin. In France, it still occurs in Aquitaine and Poitou-Charentes along undisturbed clean, well-vegetated rivers, but it is probably continuing to decline due to habitat loss, shooting and accidental poisoning from bait put out to control a rodent, the introduced Coypu (*Myocastor coypus*).

Other members of the Mustelidae include the Stoat (*M. erminea*), the rather smaller Weasel (*M. nivalis*), the striking Western Polecat (*M. putorius*), with its distinctive facial mask, the much larger, long-furred Pine Marten (*Martes martes*) and the similar Beech Marten (*M. foina*), as well as the familiar Badger (*Meles meles*). The Eurasian Otter (*Lutra lutra*) is perhaps the most popular member of the family because of its grace, agility and large size. It is wide-spread almost throughout France, except on the islands, and although it had been declining in the later 20th century due to a combination of habitat loss, pollution, competition with introduced species and other factors, numbers are currently probably more stable or increasing again.

ABOVE The Eurasian Otter is common and widespread almost throughout France, though rarely seen due to its largely nocturnal habits.
BELOW The Coypu is an introduced rodent from South America. It occurs in a number of wetlands in France despite measures to control it.

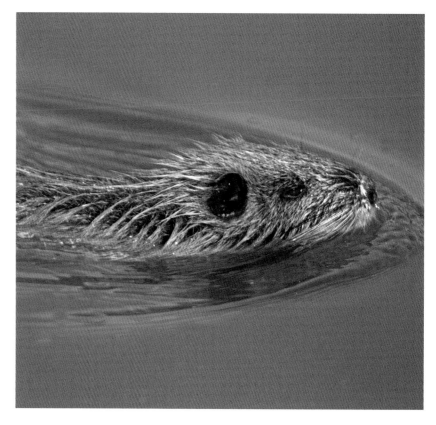

The Cat Family

The cat family, Felidae, is not well represented in France, at least not by native species. The Wildcat (*Felis silvestris*) is remarkably uncommon and local, confined to the wooded parts of the Jura and some neighbouring parts of the Alps. The much larger Lynx (*Lynx lynx*) was becoming steadily rarer in France, disappearing from the Vosges in 1830, the Massif Central in 1875, the Jura in 1885 and the Alps in 1940. The only remaining natural population is in the Pyrenees, but it is now coming back into the Jura and Alps from reintroduced populations in Switzerland, and has also been reintroduced directly into the Vosges. Hopefully, this fabulous cat may at last become common in France again in suitable areas.

Genet

An interesting cat-like animal (though actually in a different family, the Viverridae), is the Common or European Genet (*Genetta genetta*). It is widespread on the Iberian Peninsula and in much of the western part of France, as far north as Normandy, and is treated as a native species, though zoologists believe it is a very ancient introduction. It is an attractive ani-

LEFT The beautiful Wild Cat is surprisingly uncommon in France, confined to just a few wooded mountain areas in the east.
BELOW Common Seals are steadily increasing on the sandier coasts of northern France.

mal, about a metre long including the tail, rather like a spotted and striped marten, with a long tail that has black rings all along it. Genets prefer wild areas and are mainly nocturnal, so it is rare to see one except perhaps on the roads at night in optimal habitat such as the Pyrenees.

Seals

Seals, in the family Phocidae, are remarkably uncommon in France in comparison with European countries further north. The Grey Seal (*Halichoerus grypus*) is probably the most common species, but it is confined as a breeding animal to two groups of islands off the Breton coast: the Sept-Iles and the archipelago of Molènes, off the coast west of Brest, some of the most oceanic and Atlantic parts of France. Individuals can be seen more widely all down the Atlantic coast and into the English Channel. The Common Seal (*Phoca vitulina*) has a cuter, more dog-like face (compared with the 'Roman-nose' profile of the Grey Seal), and is often browner. It is becoming more common along the channel beaches of France, though perhaps just as shifting overflow outliers from the much larger populations in England and Holland. The Mediterranean Monk Seal, as mentioned above, is either very rare or extinct around Corsica, though there are reasonable hopes that it may return.

Hoofed Mammals

Wild Boar

It is not possible to describe the mammals of France without mentioning the Wild Boar (*Sus scrofa*), known as *sanglier* in French. It is the most primitive of the Artiodactyla order, which includes the deer, goats and sheep, and it bears little resemblance to most of the rest of the group. In France, Wild Boar are common and widespread wherever there are woodlands, especially where there is a good matrix of forest, grassland (including agricultural land) and water supplies. A good sign of the presence of boar is their diggings in grassland, with dozens of holes and turned-over turves in a small area, quite unlike the signs of any other mammal's activities. Wild Boar tend to be nocturnal, though females in particular can become more diurnal in autumn. In France, they are one of the most popular quarry animals for hunters, and *sanglier sauvage* is a common menu item in many restaurants.

Deer

Deer, of the family Cervidae, are abundant in France. The little Roe Deer (*Capreolus capreolus*) is widespread though rarely seen in any numbers as it is a more solitary species than most. The Fallow Deer (*Dama dama*) is now common in the north-

ABOVE, RIGHT A Grey Seal and her pup. Grey Seals are restricted as a breeding species to Brittany, though they can be seen elsewhere at times.
RIGHT The Wild Boar is a common and widespread species in France despite being a popular animal for hunting.

ABOVE A male Roe Deer looks up from feeding in its forest habitat.

ABOVE The stately Red Deer occurs in scattered forest locations through France, mainly in the north.

ern forests, mostly due to reintroductions for hunting or orna-ment. The Red Deer (*Cervus elaphus*) is a native species that does best in large forest areas, especially in hilly areas, with good populations in La Petite Pierre (Bas-Rhin), the Massif de Châteauvillain-Arc-en-Barrois (Haute-Marne), the Jura and the Compiègne Forest, north-east of Paris. The Corsican Red Deer (*C. e. corsicanus*) became extinct on Corsica in the 1960s, but has since been reintroduced into enclosures from the surviving Sardinian populations. The Sika Deer (*C. nippon*) is an intro-duced species rather like the Red Deer, but a little smaller and more spotted; it occurs in a few areas, but does not seem to be spreading much.

BELOW A Sika Deer hind – this is an introduced species from Japan that is found in scattered colonies in France.

Chamois

Perhaps the most interesting and appealing of the hoofed ani-mals are all in the Bovidae – the Chamois and related species, the Ibex (*Capra ibex*) and the Mouflon (*Ovis ammon* or *O. ori-entalis*). In France, Chamois occur as two species and a possi-ble separate subspecies. The Izard (*Rupicapra pyrenaica*), some-times just treated as a subspecies of the Chamois (*R. rupicapra*), is widespread and doing well in the high pastures and wood-lands of the Pyrenees. It resembles the Chamois, but is smaller, rather more reddish and has a whiter throat. It is replaced in the Alps by the Chamois, which can occur right up to 3,500 m in summer. Both are wonderful species to watch, incredibly agile as they move among rocks at high altitudes. In summer, you often first see them on snow patches, where they stand out more clearly as they attempt to cool off or gain a little respite from insect parasites. In the Chartreuse Mountains north of Grenoble, the Chartreuse Chamois (*R. r. cartusiana*) occurs, though it is not doing particularly well, and the recent thought-less reintroduction of the more fertile ordinary Chamois into the same mountain range does not bode well for its future.

Ibex

The story of the Ibex in Europe is well known but worth retelling. Once, Ibex were widespread throughout the moun-tain areas of Europe, common enough to be a frequent inspi-ration for cave artists, for example at Lascaux. The arrival of guns and the belief that their horns cured impotence spelled their death knell, and they quickly disappeared from their whole former range with the exception of a small part of the Italian Alps, where they were protected because it was the monarchy's private hunting preserve. Their protection in other areas followed, and in 1922 this beautiful wild area became the Gran Paradiso National Park, followed eventually by the creation of the adjacent Vanoise National Park in France in 1963.

Ibex are now doing well in many parts of the Alps, but the Vanoise-Abruzzo area retains the most important population, with around 2,000 animals in the French section out of a total of 3,000 or so in France as a whole, and perhaps 30,000 throughout Europe. Ibex are striking and attractive large mammals, very agile like most alpine species, and quite conspicuous in their open high mountain habitat. Males have long, curved, ribbed horns, up to 85 cm long in old animals, while those of females are much smaller. Their recovery from very low levels up to viable unthreatened population levels in Europe in a relatively short time gives hope for the recovery of other rare species.

ABOVE An Izard (the Pyrenean species of Chamois) feeding in high pastures in the Pyrenees.

BELOW A majestic male Ibex resting in the high pastures of the Vanoise National Park.

ABOVE The appealing Alpine Marmot is once again quite common in the higher mountains of France.

Mouflon

Finally, the Mouflon is the only wild sheep in Europe, though it is not a genuinely wild species. It appears to have been introduced into Europe during Neolithic times and to have subsequently gone wild, while evolving to an extent away from the original Asian populations, producing a rather confused taxonomy. European mouflons are generally known as the Mediterranean Mouflon, and in France the largest population can be found in the Massif du Caroux Espinouse, in the Haut-Languedoc Natural Regional Park (with an estimated 1,500–2,000 animals, mainly in a no-hunting reserve), though there are smaller populations in the Cévennes, the Savoie mountains, Corsica and elsewhere.

Rodents

There is not enough space to describe the many rodent (order Rodentia) species in France, but two in particular are worth a special mention.

Red Squirrel

The delightful Red Squirrel (*Sciurus vulgaris*) is common almost throughout France, especially in areas of coniferous woodland, where it feeds on pine nuts, buds and other vegetable matter, only occasionally turning to birds' eggs or invertebrates – generally speaking it is a welcome part of the countryside. By contrast, the introduced Grey Squirrel (*S. carolinensis*) is a serious problem. At the moment, it is not present in France (apart from the odd unconfirmed record in the Alps), but there is great concern about its imminent arrival as populations in northern Italy spread inexorably northwards and westwards. At least there is

time for the French authorities to plan for its arrival, using the experience of Britain and elsewhere, in the hope of limiting or preventing its spread.

Alpine Marmot

The Alpine Marmot (*Marmota marmota*) is a lovely animal, much the biggest of France's rodents, with a body weight of up to 4.5 kg and a nose to tail length of up to 70 cm. Marmots live in loose colonies in alpine pastures above the tree-line up to about 3,000 m, or in clearings, where they may become very abundant in good conditions. They are almost exclusively diurnal, apart from in very hot weather, so they are readily seen by most visitors to the Alps. They also have a loud, high-pitched, repeated whistle, audible from over a kilometre away. In some places, for instance around ski stations, they become quite tame and start to depend on food from visitors. There was a time when they were seriously endangered in France, but a combination of protection, reintroduction and a more enlightened attitude has allowed them to become common again almost throughout the Alps and Pyrenees.

Cetaceans: the Whales and Dolphins

Of all mammals, the cetaceans are the most adapted for an aquatic life. They are structurally suited to propulsion through water, much better at using oxygen than land mammals, and have highly adapted means of communicating and perception through sonar and echolocation. As a group, their numbers have suffered heavily in recent centuries, through severe over-exploitation, pollution and accidental deaths as a result of fishing for other species or collision with boats. A less obvious but equally devastating problem that is only now becoming understood is that of noise pollution. The noise generated by ships,

BELOW The Common Dormouse (*Muscardinus avellanarius*) is one of the most attractive of the small rodents, to be found in wooded areas throughout France.

ABOVE The huge Sperm Whale can occasionally be seen off the coasts of France wherever the water is deep enough.

military use (especially active sonar) and devices such as seal scarers not only severely interrupts cetaceans' communication systems, but is also seriously implicated in mass strandings, deviations from normal migration routes, severe haemorrhaging and potentially fatal decompression sickness when animals are forced to surface too quickly. In some cases, numbers of cetaceans are beginning to rise again as the problems are better understood, and commercial whaling is generally banned, though many problems remain.

About 20 species of cetacean regularly appear in French waters, with examples from each of the two main orders – the toothed whales and dolphins (Odontoceti), and the baleen whales (Mysticeti), the latter of which includes all the 'great whales'. The baleen whales, such as the Minke Whale (*Balaenoptera acutorostra*), are very rare in French waters and hardly ever seen anywhere near land, since they generally move further west and north. There are many more species of Odontoceti, and these are more likely to be seen. The list includes porpoises, several dolphins, the Killer Whale or Orca (*Orcinus orca*) – the largest of the dolphins – the Long-finned Pilot Whale (*Globicephala melaena*), the species most often involved in the mass strandings of whales on coasts, and even Sperm Whales (*Physeter macrocephalus*), though it is the dolphins and porpoises that are most likely to be seen.

The Bottle-nosed Dolphin (*Tursiops truncatus*), or *grand dauphin* in French, is quite common in both Atlantic and Mediterranean waters, and is the most frequently seen cetacean in the French Mediterranean. Up to 4 m long, it is larger than the Common Dolphin (*Delphinus delphis*) or Striped Dolphin (*Stenella coeruleoalba),* both of which reach about 2.5 m in length, are similarly wide-ranging and are also often seen in the Mediterranean. A recent multinational initiative has provided for the establishment of a 'cetacean sanctuary' – Pelagos – in the Ligurian Sea, between southern France, Italy and Corsica. This aims to reduce the threats to cetaceans (and other marine animals like turtles and seals) here, and allow their population levels to rise. All three of the dolphin species can be seen here.

The rather similar Harbour Porpoise (*Phocoena phocoena*) is actually in a different family from the dolphins (the Phocoenidae rather than the Delphinidae). It is less social and less prone to leaping out of the water and is therefore less frequently seen. It is essentially an Atlantic coastal species that does enter the Mediterranean but is clearly less at home there. It is most often seen off the Channel and north-western coasts.

Organized cetacean-watching trips are possible in French waters. The Breton coasts are good for dolphins, Harbour Porpoises and some other species, with tours available at most of the major ports such as Brest or Lorient. The most westerly of the ferry routes to the British Isles, especially Roscoff to Plymouth or Roscoff to Cork, can provide excellent watching possibilities. The establishment of the Pelagos sanctuary has spawned quite an industry of whale- and dolphin-watching tours in the Mediterranean, from ports such as St Mandrier (Toulon), St Raphaël (near Frèjus), Monaco and L'Ile-Rousse on the north Corsican coast.

Chapter 7
REPTILES AND AMPHIBIANS

This chapter describes some of the other important vertebrates of France, the reptiles and amphibians (collectively known as the herpetofauna), which play such an important part in the country's ecology. These two major animal classes are linked by the fact that both comprise cold-blooded vertebrates without the ability to regulate their body temperature internally. Reptiles and amphibians are more primitive than mammals and are limited in the sense that they are unable to be active under cold conditions, where their body temperature falls too low, though conversely, because they do not need a regular food intake to maintain body temperature, they can survive for long periods without food. In fact, there are few practical limitations on where they can occur in a country like France, and they can be found up to very high elevations in the mountains, surviving despite many months of cold and snow.

LEFT A vividly coloured Stripeless Tree Frog clings
precariously to a rock face.

ABOVE A curious group of Common Frogs in the Maritime Alps, all
facing outwards with one more on the top.

R EPTILES ARE SCALY, DRY-SKINNED AND ABLE TO SURVIVE in very
hot locations. Amphibians are non-scaly, moist-skinned
and mostly confined to humid locations with some link to
water for their breeding period, though there are exceptions.

Amphibians

The amphibians of France are something special. Their numbers and diversity may not compare with those of wet tropical
countries such as Borneo and Costa Rica – for this is the epicentre of amphibian diversity – but in a purely European con-
text, their numbers are remarkable. There are over 40 species
of amphibian in France and (perhaps more significantly) there
is a higher proportion of endemics or near-endemics than in
any other major group – roughly 25 per cent, depending upon
how widely the definition of endemic is drawn. Due to its
diversity of habitats and climates, and central position with
access to the Iberian and Italian Peninsulas, as well as eastern
and northern Europe, France has more species of amphibian
than any other European country. By comparison, the British
Isles have only six native amphibians (with one or two more
that are subject to controversy), of which none is endemic.

The last few decades have seen a great deal of work on the
taxonomy and ecology of European amphibians, and many
new species have been discovered or separated out. For the
naturalist, amphibians are a fascinating but often rather difficult group, because some of the species distinctions are hard
to apply in the field without specialized knowledge, though of
course they can be enjoyed without detailed identification.
Many are at least partially diurnal – those that are not can often
be readily heard at night – and they frequently occur in quite
large numbers, so they are likely to come to the attention of
most naturalists.

Salamanders and Newts

The salamanders and newts (belonging mainly to the family
Salamandridae, with one member of the cave salamander family, Plethodontidae) are probably the most poorly known group
of amphibians. The single species of cave salamander that
occurs in France is Ambrosi's Cave Salamander (*Hydromantes
strinatii*). It is found in the Maritime Alps on both sides of the
border with Italy (with an introduced population in the Ariège
region of the Pyrenees). These salamanders are lungless, carrying out all their oxygen exchange through the skin, so it is
hardly surprising that they favour highly humid, cool environments such as caves, though they are by no means confined to
them. In the Maritime Alps, they are almost always on limestone, in any habitat rich in caves, fissures and overhanging
shaded rocks, right up to an altitude of 2,000 m.

The remaining salamanders and newts all belong to the family Salamandridae. The best known is almost certainly the Fire Salamander (*Salamandra salamandra*). Due to its striking combination of shiny black and yellow markings and its slow progress over the ground it is more easily seen than many species. Although primarily nocturnal, particularly in hot, dry weather, it is also active in wet or humid weather, and may often be seen in these conditions, foraging on the woodland floor. It is widespread throughout virtually the whole of France, though generally most common in hilly, wooded districts, reaching to altitudes of well over 2,000 m in the Pyrenees, where most individuals are considered to belong to a separate subspecies.

The rather similar Corsican Fire Salamander (*S. corsica*) is wholly endemic to the island of Corsica, where it fills essentially the same niche, and the Fire Salamander (of which it was considered to be a subspecies until recently) is absent. The Alpine Salamander (*S. atra*) is rather like an all-black Fire Salamander. It is widespread in the Alps but confined in France to the Haute-Savoie area, where its exact status is now rather uncertain since some populations have been separated out as the endemic Lanza's Alpine Salamander. These two species are both mountain specialists, occurring up to and often beyond the tree-line, and distinctive in giving birth to live young – perhaps an adaptation to the short alpine season.

Two species of brook newt or brook salamander (*Euproctus* spp.) are found in France, both endemics of limited range – the Pyrenean Brook Newt (*Euproctus*, or *Calotriton*, *asper*), which is widespread at higher altitudes in the Pyrenees, and the Corsican Brook Newt (*E. montanus*). Both species are rather inconspicuous, brownish and aquatic, and live very long lives (up to 26 years has been recorded) in cold mountain streams and ponds.

There are six species of pond newt in France, all belonging to the genus *Triturus*. Most are widespread species occurring throughout much of Europe, but the Marbled Newt (*T. marmoratus*) is worth a special mention because it is a particularly large species (up to 17 cm long in the largest females), boldly marbled with green and black, and topped with a fine crest in breeding-condition males. It is also a south-west European endemic confined to southern and western France and the Iberian Peninsula.

Toads and Frogs

The remaining amphibians in France all belong to the group Anura, or tailless amphibians. In English, there is a simple separation of these into frogs and toads, but this actually reflects the fact that in the

ABOVE The dazzling Fire Salamander is surprisingly rarely seen because it is almost exclusively nocturnal, although it is common in France.

species-poor populations of Britain, there *is* a simple separation: the frogs that are found in Britain are more graceful, more likely to jump and have wetter, smoother skins than French frogs, while Britain's toads are stout, squat, warty and more likely to walk. In France, a much greater variety of species exists, and many cannot readily be assigned to either one or other group.

The Discoglossidae family contains the midwife toads, painted frogs and fire-bellied toads, representatives of all of which occur in France. The Common Midwife Toad (*Alytes obstetricans*) is a delightful little species, often heard but rarely seen. The adults are small, rarely more than 5 cm long, and normally crepuscular or nocturnal, so you are only likely to

BELOW The Pyrenean Brook Newt is confined to watery areas in the higher parts of the Pyrenees.

come across them if they are disturbed by chance under a paving stone, log or similar place.

These toads tend to live in loose colonies often comprising many hundreds of individuals, which collectively make a wonderfully symphonic 'wall of sound'. Although the individual call is just a single short, melodic note (rather like the call of a Scops Owl, *Otus scops*, or a sonar pulse), because many individuals call at once and the notes are all different depending on the size and age of the individual, the net effect is remarkable. Even the females join in during the mating period. The reason why they are called 'midwife' toads (though perhaps it should be 'midhusband toads'!) is that the males wrap the string of eggs around their rear end and carry it everywhere, always keeping it cool and moist, even travelling to open water if necessary. Females choose the larger males (recognizable even in the dark by their deeper voices) and a successful male may mate with several females, though the more eggs he is carrying, the lower his chances of an additional mating.

The painted frogs (*Discoglossus* spp.) are an intriguing little group of frogs, occurring nowadays in vestiges of a formerly more widespread range. They are small and boldly marked (definitely looking 'painted' in some individuals), with roughly circular pupils unlike the horizontal pupils of most typical frogs. The Painted Frog (*D. pictus*) is essentially an African species, introduced to south-west France in about 1900 and now relatively widespread in that area. The two native painted frogs are the Corsican Painted Frog (*D. montalentii*), which is endemic just to Corsica, where it is found almost throughout the uplands; and the Tyrrhenian Frog (*D. sardus*), which is endemic to a number of islands to the west of Italy and occurs on Corsica at generally lower elevations.

The two species of spadefoot (*Pelobates* spp.) are closely related to the painted frogs, though they have vertical pupils and prominent, sharp-edged, spade-like projections on their hind feet, which account for their remarkable ability to dig themselves quickly into a hole, or to retreat to as deep as a metre in periods of drought. The Common Spadefoot (*P. fuscus*) is an eastern European species that just reaches into eastern France, with an isolated population in the Brenne area. The Western Spadefoot (*P. cultripes*) is a south-west European endemic rather larger than the Common Spadefoot and with a black 'spade'. Both are quite large, up to 11 cm long, and with enormous tadpoles that can also reach 10 or 11 cm long!

There are three native species of typical toad (*Bufo* spp.) in France. The Common Toad (*B. bufo*) is common everywhere

TOP, LEFT A large, boldly marked example of the Common Toad high in the French Alps.

CENTRE, LEFT A Natterjack Toad in its breeding pool. This species is mainly nocturnal, although the noisy breeding colonies can be heard from up to a kilometre away.

BOTTOM, LEFT The attractively marbled Green Toad is a rare species in France, just reaching into the easternmost parts of the country.

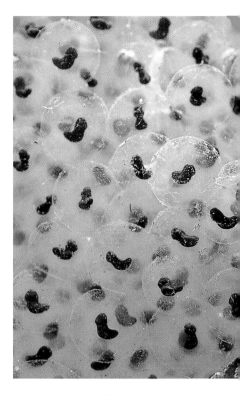

and generally well known, though the Natterjack Toad (*B. calamita*) is much more easily overlooked. Natterjacks, though widespread, are declining, and tend to occur in colonies where there are warm, shallow lakes, for example among dunes and in old quarries. They are mainly nocturnal and do not generally come into gardens or towns, so they are rarely seen, though they can travel several kilometres in search of food, apparently using the Earth's magnetic field to navigate by. The third species, the Green Toad (*B. viridis*) is much rarer, confined to the extreme east of France and to Corsica, where it is quite common. It is a highly distinctive toad, boldly marked with green patches on a greyish or orange-flushed background, though you can often locate it first by its very distinctive call – a high-pitched, rapid repetition of a single note for about 10 seconds, sounding almost like a miniature pump from a distance, and more likely to be confused with an insect than any other amphibian.

One tends to think of tree frogs as an entirely tropical group – and so they are, mainly, with almost 1,000 species found in the tropics, but three species are also found in France. They are all rather similar in appearance and occur in the same habitats and, while they are not normally found in trees, they are almost always off the ground in tall vegetation such as reeds, thistles, tamarisks and so on. They are small, beautiful little frogs only about 4 cm long, but usually bright shiny emerald green. Despite this, they can be very difficult to see, and are often best located by their calls.

The Common Tree Frog (*Hyla arborea*) occurs commonly over most of France in suitable habitats, except for the southeast. It is generally replaced in the south by the Stripeless Tree Frog (*H. meridionalis*), and the two overlap in south-west France. On Corsica, there is a third species, the Tyrrhenian Tree

ABOVE, LEFT The little Common Tree Frog can be found almost throughout France, except in parts of the south, where it is replaced by the Stripeless Tree Frog.
ABOVE, CENTRE A Stripeless Tree Frog in the Camargue. The stripe through the eye does not extend along the flanks.
ABOVE, RIGHT The spawn of a Common Frog, with the eggs just beginning to develop a recognizable shape.

Frog (*H. sarda*), endemic to the Tyrrhenian Sea area, which is probably most closely related to the Common Tree Frog. The Common and Tyrrhenian Tree Frogs have harsh, loud, chacking calls, with a regularly repeated note, audible from a long way off if there is a large colony. In fact, the production of this loud call by the males is so expensive in effort that some males simply sit next to very loud males and do not call themselves, in the hope of being confused with a more potent male by the female when she arrives! The Stripeless Tree Frog has a quieter, more resonant and deeper call, which has been confused with the call of the Corncrake.

Finally, there are the true frogs, all of which belong to the genus *Rana*, though they are usually divided into the noisy, very aquatic and often diurnal green frogs, and the quieter, more terrestrial and nocturnal brown frogs. Almost all visitors to the countryside of France will be familiar with the green frogs, even if it is only because they have heard the series of 'plops' as the frogs leave their sunbathing spots and leap back into the water when disturbed.

There are actually five green frogs, plus hybrids and introductions, and they are often rather difficult to separate, especially in view of continuing research and discussion. The Marsh Frog (*R. ridibunda*) is the largest and generally least green of these, native only in the east of France (at the western

ABOVE A large Pool Frog, one of the frog species considered to be edible in France.

ABOVE An Edible Frog basking on the leaves of a Yellow Water Lily in the evening sun.

edge of its European range) but widely introduced elsewhere in France. The Pool Frog (*R. lessonae*) and the Edible Frog (*R. esculenta*) are extremely similar, and hard to identify with certainty in the absence of specialist knowledge. In the northern two-thirds of France, one or other of these is much the most

likely green frog to be encountered. Not surprisingly, both of these species are considered to be edible, as well as a number of other species.

In south-west France the dominant green frog is the Iberian Water Frog (*R. perezi*), which is similar to the above, but gener-

INDRE'S HERPETOFAUNA

To give a more immediate feel for the richness of herpetofauna in France locally, this is a complete list of the amphibians and reptiles found in one department, Indre, in the centre of France.

Reptiles
European Pond Terrapin (*Emys orbicularis*)
Slow Worm (*Anguis fragilis*)
Sand Lizard (*Lacerta agilis*)
Green Lizard (*L. viridis*)
Common Wall Lizard (*Podarcis muralis*)
Western Whip Snake (*Coluber viridiflavus*)
Smooth Snake (*Coronella austriaca*)
Viperine Snake (*Natrix maura*)
Grass Snake (*N. natrix*)
Aesculapian Snake (*Elaphe longissima*)
Asp Viper (*Vipera aspic*)
Adder (*V. berus*)

Amphibians
Fire Salamander (*Salamandra salamandra*)
Alpine Newt (*Triturus alpestris*)
Northern Crested Newt (*T. cristatus*)

Marbled Newt (*T. marmoratus*)
Palmate Newt (*T. helveticus*)
Common Newt (*T. vulgaris*)
Hybrid newt (*T.* x *blasii*, Marbled Newt x Northern Crested Newt)
Common Midwife Toad (*Alytes obstetricans*)
Common Spadefoot (*Pelobates fuscus*)
Parsley Frog (*Pelodytes punctatus*)
Yellow-bellied Toad (*Bombina variegata*)
Common Toad (*Bufo bufo*)
Natterjack Toad (*B. calamita*)
Common Tree Frog (*Hyla arborea*)
Pool Frog (*Rana lessonae*)
Edible Frog (*R. esculenta*)
Common Frog (*R. temporaria*)
Agile Frog (*R. dalmatina*)

Introduced Species
Red-eared Terrapin (*Trachemys scripta*)
Spur-thighed Tortoise (*Testudo graeca*)
Hermann's Tortoise (*T. hermanni*)
Marsh Frog (*Rana ridibunda*)

ABOVE An Iberian Water Frog (endemic to south-west France and the Iberian Peninsula) warming up after a cool night.

ABOVE Pond Terrapins are common over most of France except the north, where the winters are too cold.

ally rather less bright green and barely overlapping in its geographical range (although there is also a common hybrid, *R. grafi*, which occurs wherever the parents, Marsh and Iberian Water Frogs, are found). On Corsica, the only native green frog is the Italian Pool Frog (*R. bergeri*), which is otherwise confined to Italy.

It is worth mentioning that in addition to all the normal threats of drainage, pollution, development and so on (see Chapter 9), amphibians in France are currently faced with the devastating threat of a worldwide disease of amphibians, *Batrachochytrium dendrobatidis*, Bd. The disease, originally from South Africa, is spreading rapidly, exacerbated by global warming and the release of non-native amphibians into the countryside. So far in France it is not a serious problem, with only introduced American Bullfrogs (*R. catesbiana*) being affected, though it is known to affect species such as the Midwife Toad, Common Toad and Pool Frog elsewhere in Europe.

Reptiles

Excluding the sea turtles, which may often pass through French waters but never breed in them, there are about 35 native reptiles in France – more than most people might imagine, and certainly more than most people will have seen. Typically, they are both more abundant and more diverse in the southern parts of the country, and most of them have a hibernation period to a greater or lesser extent.

Tortoises and Terrapins
One of the three European species of tortoise can be found in France – this is Hermann's Tortoise (*Testudo hermanni*). It is naturally restricted to areas with hot summers and mild winters, but in France it is further restricted by habitat loss, fire, dogs and many other factors, and only occurs now on the mainland in the Massif des Maures (inland from St Tropez), and

BELOW An adult Hermann's Tortoise in the open woodlands of the Massif des Maures, the species' stronghold in France.

ABOVE Slow Worms are very common throughout most of France in a wide range of habitats.

BELOW A young Ocellated Lizard – this very large lizard species is confined to the far south in France.

BOTTOM The delightful little Common Wall Lizard occurs throughout France in a wide variety of colour forms.

the extreme south-west of France on the Spanish border, though this latter population may be extinct. On Corsica, this species is still widespread in the lowlands, and there is evidence that this population is gradually diverging from that of the mainland in colour and shape, though not yet sufficiently to be given taxonomic status. The species can be found in a variety of habitats, but it occurs most commonly in open woodland, scrub and rough grassland.

If you are in the right area, these tortoises are best discovered by listening for the rustle of their movement, especially before about midday, when they are most active. In the Massif des Maures there is a tortoise conservation centre, the Village des Tortues (www.villagetortues.com), near Gonfaron, which is dedicated to tortoises and well worth a visit, and there is now a similar one on Corsica at Moltifau.

The terrapins are closely related aquatic reptiles. The European Pond Terrapin (*Emis orbicularis*) is markedly limited by both summer warmth and winter cold, and only occurs in south and south-west France to about as far north as the Brenne. In the warm post-glacial period it occurred much further north, including in Britain, so it may well move north again as the climate warms. These are diurnal creatures that spend much of the time sunbathing on logs or on the water's surface, though they are usually quite timid unless they are habituated to the presence of humans. The Spanish Terrapin (*Mauremys leprosa*) is similar but paler, with fewer yellow spots and yellowish stripes on the neck. Within France it has a very restricted distribution, just creeping over the Spanish border into the Massif des Albères area, south of Perpignan.

Lizards and Skinks

The group Sauria includes all the lizards and skinks, of which there are about 20 species in France. Some, such as the Slow Worm (*Anguis fragilis*), Viviparous Lizard (*Lacerta vivipara*), Common Wall Lizard (*Podarcis muralis*) and Western Green Lizard (*Lacerta bilineata*), are widespread through most of France. Of these, the Western Green Lizard (formerly included in the Green Lizard, but now considered a separate species) is the most distinctive. It is a large diurnal animal – up to 40 cm long, including the tail – bright emerald green flecked with black, and the males have an attractive blue throat patch. It lives in various habitats, but most commonly in woodland edges and grassland with scattered rocks or bushes for cover, particularly over limestone. It disappears at the slightest sign of a threat, and climbs quite readily if there is no other cover, but will usually soon reappear if the sun is out.

A close relative of the green lizards is the Ocellated Lizard (*Lacerta lepida* or *Timon lepidus*), easily the largest lizard in France, reaching up to 90 cm in the largest individuals, though 60 cm is more normal. Apart from its size, it is easily distinguishable by its massive head and the presence of large blue spots along its flanks. It is strongly warmth dependent and therefore confined to Mediterranean France and the south-ernmost parts of the Atlantic coast in warm, open habitats such as scrub and *garrigue*, and the open plains of La Crau, east of the Camargue (though Ocellated Lizards have declined drastically here, maybe due to a disease).

Among the remaining lizards of France, there are no species that are completely confined to France, though several almost are. In the Pyrenees there is a group of closely related rock lizards that occur in limited areas on either side of the French–Spanish border. They are all typical rock lizards, differing from each other, and from the more widespread Iberian Rock Lizard (*Lacerta monticola*), in relatively small details. All of this group are often placed in the genus *Iberolacerta* with the same specific names.

The Pyrenean Rock Lizard (*Lacerta bonnali*) occurs in the high Pyrenees, with its French population centred around the Lac Bleu de Bigorre, north-west of the Col du Tourmalet. This is a restricted high-altitude species occurring at up to 3,000 m, with a rather short season of activity and a correspondingly long hibernation period. Aurelio's Rock Lizard (*L. aurelioi*) has an even more restricted distribution, around the area where Andorra, Spain and France all meet, at the same sort of altitudes, and it is best distinguished by its geographical range. The third species, the Aran Rock Lizard (*L. aranica*), has the most restricted range of all, currently known from just 26 sq km of the Maubermé Massif in the Central Pyrenees, east of Bagnères de Luchon, where it occurs at heights of between 1,900 and 2,500 m. These last two species were not described until 1994 and 1993 respectively.

As usual, Corsica has its fair share of endemic species, though none is confined to Corsica alone. Among the lizards there are two Tyrrhenian endemics (restricted to the islands of

ABOVE The large and distinctive Western Green Lizard is widespread throughout France in warm habitats with ample cover.

the Tyrrhenian Sea, notably Corsica and Sardinia). There is the delightfully named Pygmy Algyroides (*Algyroides fitzingeri*), a rather dull-brownish lizard that is undistinguished apart from its small size (around 4 cm excluding the tail) and its preference for relatively shaded habitats. By contrast, Bedriaga's Rock Lizard (*Lacerta,* or *Archaeolacerta, bedriagae*) is an attractive, largish lizard, boldly reticulated with grey-green and black, which occurs in montane habitats and is especially common at heights of around 2,000 m where the vegetation starts to thin out.

BELOW An intricately patterned Tyrrhenian Wall Lizard (*Podarcis tiliguerta*) in the mountains of Corsica.

TOP A Moorish Gecko basking in the sun in spring, before it becomes too hot.

ABOVE This young Turkish Gecko is watching for insects at night on the wall of a house near an outside light.

ABOVE, RIGHT A Western Whip Snake emerges from its burrow in the Brenne area.

There is also a Tyrrhenian endemic gecko, the European Leaf-toed Gecko (*Euleptes europaea*), which occurs within France on Corsica and several islands just off the south-east mainland, such as the Iles d'Hyères. Like other geckoes it has adhesive pads on its feet, but they are restricted to the toes in this species, and it has a smooth skin without the warts of other geckoes. Unlike the other two geckoes in France – the Turkish Gecko (*Hemidactylus turcicus*) and Moorish Gecko (*Tarentola mauritanica*) – it rarely associates with humans or comes into houses, and is most often found in rock crevices and drystone walls, where due to its nocturnal habits it is hardly ever seen. Few people realize that geckoes have quite loud calls, and this species makes a pleasant '*tsi-tsi-tsi*' sound.

Snakes

Finally, on to many people's least favourite reptiles, the snakes or Ophidia, of which there are 12 species in France. None is confined to France alone, though Seoane's Viper (*Vipera seoanei*) lives in a very restricted area of northern Spain and Portugal, just reaching into France at the far south-western corner, where the Pyrenees meet the Atlantic Ocean.

The most widespread species of snake in France are the Smooth Snake (*Coronella austriaca*), Adder (*Vipera berus*), Asp Viper (*V. aspis*), Grass Snake (*Natrix natrix*) and Viperine Snake

(*N. Maura*). Of these species, only the Grass Snake can be found throughout France. Within France, Asp Vipers are probably more common and widespread than Adders, especially in the southern half of the country, though the two are often confused. The Asp Viper has slightly more interrupted markings on the back (though both are variable), and it has a definite small, upwards projection on its snout (though nothing like as distinct as that of the Nose-horned Viper, *Vipera ammodytes*, which occurs further east than France); both are venomous, though it is extremely rare for the bite to be fatal. Interestingly, the toxicity of the venom is known to vary within the geographical range, and Asp Vipers from south-west France have the most potent venom.

The Montpellier Snake (*Malpolon monspessulanus*) is the longest and largest of French snakes. A fully grown large adult can be around 2 m long (occasionally up to 2.5 m) and weigh up to 3 kg – a formidable opponent. As its common name suggests, it is essentially a Mediterranean species, common in *garrigue* and other open, warm habitats with some cover. It is a diurnal hunter with an unwise preference for sunbathing on the warm tarmac of roads; it is easily the most common snake road casualty in southern France. Its enormous size and aggressive behaviour make it the dominant snake where it does occur, and it tends to eat any other snakes it finds, as well as lizards. Although it is venomous, it is back-fanged and thus unlikely to bite humans – no one is known to have ever been killed by a Montpellier Snake. As one of its adaptations to living in such a warm, dry environment it produces an oil from a gland close to its nostril, which is wiped over its body. This is believed to waterproof the skin and reduce desiccation, though it may also serve a sexual function.

ABOVE Adders are familiar snakes to anyone who regularly walks in the countryside, especially in spring when they bask in the sun.
RIGHT Grass Snakes frequently take to the water in spring and early summer in search of tadpoles and young amphibians.
BELOW, RIGHT A young Viperine Snake in a Provencal stream. These are the most aquatic of French snakes.

The Western Whip Snake (*Coluber viridiflavus*) is probably the most frequently seen snake species over most of France (except in roughly the northern quarter, from which it is absent). These snakes are large (up to 1.5 m long), very active, boldly marked with black and yellow, generally common where they do occur and often come into contact with humans in gardens, at picnic sites, on fishing lakes and so on.

One of the more appealing of snakes is the Viperine Snake (*Natrix maura*), which may look rather like a slender Adder, but has quite different habits. It is the most aquatic of the French snakes, spending most of its time in or around water, and able to swim for long periods or even to remained submerged for a quarter of an hour or more. It hunts tadpoles, small amphibians, and even large aquatic insects, using sight, scent and touch to find prey. Viperine Snakes are often seen when moving slowly among the weeds in a river.

Orsini's Viper is a little-known species, but it is of interest because it is the only mountain specialist among French snakes. It is a small, slender, rather docile viper with weak venom, found at altitudes of more than 1,000 m, and up as high as 2,500 m, in the Maritime Alps and nearby areas. It feeds mainly on lizards, small mammals and fledgling birds, and frequently turns to grasshoppers when these become abundant in late summer.

Chapter 8
INVERTEBRATE LIFE

In this chapter we take a look at some of the invertebrates of France. The number of invertebrate species that occur in the country is not known precisely, but as France lies in such a central position within Europe and has such an enormous range of habitats, it has a very high proportion of European species – the total number of insects alone is estimated at about 40,000 species. Since it is clearly impractical to cover this vast range of species (many of which are small, nocturnal or little known), this chapter focuses on the better-known and more visible representatives, such as butterflies, moths, dragonflies and damselflies, and other major groups.

LEFT The Broad-bordered Bee Hawkmoth is a highly active, day-flying species – here it is feeding on a Meadow Thistle.

ABOVE The Scarce Swallowtail butterfly, with its distinctive zebra-like wing pattern.

ABOVE Grizzled skippers 'mud puddling' together in a group in the Maritime Alps in summer.

THE TREMENDOUS DIVERSITY AND NUMBERS of invertebrate species by far outweigh all the vertebrate groups put together. It is well known that the tropics have the greatest variety, numbers and sheer exuberance of invertebrates, with an extraordinary range of forms and adaptations in a vast number of species. France itself is large enough to have detectable geographical trends within its invertebrate diversity, and the number of species increases towards the south and decreases towards the north. This is partly due to the fact that the temperatures are higher in the south, but other factors come into play here, particularly the greater intensity of agriculture and habitat loss in the north.

Butterflies

Butterflies probably fulfil most people's idea of attractive and interesting insects. They are quite large, active in the day, generally colourful, usually harmless and certainly non-biting, as well as being readily identifiable, so it is hardly surprising that they are the best-known and most popular insect group. Of the 420 or so species of butterfly known in Europe (depending upon how you define Europe), about 250 species are found in France (depending on how you define species, and which records you accept). Among them there is a wonderful range of colours and forms, from tiny brown skippers to large and colourful species such as the extraordinary Two-tailed Pasha (*Charaxes jasius*) and the graceful Scarce Swallowtail (*Iphiclides podalirius*), which is actually not so very scarce and looks rather like 'a flying piano', as someone once described it to me, with its bold pattern of black and white bands.

Most of the French butterfly species occur elsewhere in Europe, and there is virtually no true endemism. Many French species have a very restricted distribution, but they also occur outside French state limits. For example, there are several special Corsican species, but all also occur on the Italian island of Sardinia – thus they can be described as Tyrrhenian endemics, but not as French endemics. Even the Gavarnie Blue (*Agriades pyrenaicus*), named after a small French central Pyrenean village, is by no means a French endemic, with populations in northern Spain, the Balkans and even western Asia. In a recent study it was considered that 26 species of butterfly in France (about 10 per cent of the total species) are seriously threatened and in urgent need of attention. Interestingly, France has significant populations (defined here as being more than 15 per cent of the European total population) of only six species of butterfly.

All butterflies are beautiful, but within the 250 or so species in France there are some special gems. The skipper family (Hesperiidae) is quite large, but the species are small and frequently only noticed by specialists. One occasion when they do become noticeable, though, is when they gather to mud puddle. In warm weather, and particularly in mountain areas such as the Maritime Alps, huge numbers of butterflies gather together on wet, nutrient-rich bare soil. One of the most abundant groups to do this is the skippers, especially the various grizzled skippers (*Pyrgus* spp.). This activity, which is wonderful to watch (especially when large numbers of blues are present as well), is not fully understood, but it clearly relates to the butterflies' need for liquid in the drier climatic areas. However, the explanation is not quite as simple as that, since almost all of the visitors to mud puddles are males, and it is thought that the activity probably relates to their particular need for sodium in the reproductive process, specifically in the production of spermatophores that accompany the sperm.

The swallowtail family (Papilionidae) is quite small, with only nine species in France and about 500 worldwide, but it contains some of the most strikingly beautiful butterflies in the

ABOVE A female Clouded Apollo butterfly in the Pyrenees, resting during egg-laying.

ABOVE The Southern Festoon is a lovely and distinctive butterfly, found mainly in Mediterranean France.

apollos, swallowtails and festoons. There are three species of apollo, most notably the Mountain Apollo (*Parnassius apollo*), a large, essentially white species, but with bold red and black dots, and a wingspan of up to 8 cm. It is an inherently beautiful species, but its cachet is increased by its occurrence in spectacular higher mountain areas above about 500 m, and on up as high as 2,700 m. In France it is still common and occasionally abundant in the Alps and Pyrenees, with smaller populations in the Massif Central and Jura, though it has disappeared from the Vosges, *causses* and other areas. In the high central Pyrenees, it is common enough to be frequently seen in the streets of the higher towns and villages, such as Gavarnie.

Two very similar species of festoon occur in France – the Southern Festoon (*Zerynthia polyxena*) and the Spanish Festoon (*Z. rumina*) – both confined to the Mediterranean area. They are boldly marked black, red, white and yellow species, giving the appearance of having been scribbled on!

The remaining four species are the swallowtails, named as such because they have long 'tails' on each of their hindwings. The so-called Scarce Swallowtail is common and widespread, and very distinctive – large and with bold black vertical stripes on a white background, partly fringed with blue dots. The Common Swallowtail (*Papilio machaon*) is similarly large, but creamy yellow with more transverse black marks. There is also a Corsican Swallowtail (*P. hospiton*), which is a Tyrrhenian endemic. All of the swallowtails (and a number of other butterflies) go in

for the practice of 'hill-topping', where large numbers of butterflies gather together on suitable hilltops. These individuals are almost all males, and females simply visit until they have found a mate, then depart. These are highly charged events, with a good deal of displaying going on, and much releasing of scent.

The white family (Pieridae) is an important group with many attractive species. It contains the familiar 'cabbage

BELOW A newly emerged Common Swallowtail butterfly about to take its maiden flight.

TOP A male of the vibrantly coloured Moroccan Orange-tip feeding on the Common Centaury.
ABOVE A Large Blue butterfly in the Maritime Alps.

TOP A male Osiris Blue butterfly resting on Sainfoin, its main food plant, in the Vercors Mountains.
ABOVE The Mountain Alcon Blue lays its eggs visibly and rather randomly on the upper leaves of the Cross Gentian (*Gentiana cruciata*).

whites' but also a range of rarer whites, the clouded yellows, orange-tips and brimstones. The most striking of the whites is the Black-veined White (*Aporia crataegi*), which is common throughout most of France. It can occasionally reach pest proportions when it finds a cherry, peach or apple orchard to its liking (the larvae feed on various shrubs and trees in the rose family including the crops, but also on Blackthorn, Rowan, *Sorbus aucuparia*, and other wild species). This is a largish species, with a wingspan of about 6 cm, white but boldly marked with a complex pattern of black veins that is readily distinguishable when seen well, and often occurring in huge numbers, especially in mountain areas.

The Orange-tip (*Anthocharis cardamines*) is a common and well-known species, but in the southern parts of France there is a rather striking close relative, the Moroccan Orange-tip (*A. euphenoides*), which has bright yellow wings tipped with orange – a distinctive and beautiful combination. There are also five species of clouded yellow in France, and two species of brimstone. They include the beautiful common and widespread Brimstone (*Gonepteryx rhamni*), which is thought to be the original 'butter fly', with the male's glorious large, butter-yellow wings, and its more striking relative, confined to the southern half of the country, the Cleopatra (*G. cleopatra*). This

is rather similar to the Brimstone, but the males have a bold orange splash of colour on their forewings that is readily visible even in flight.

The Lycaenidae, containing the blues, hairstreaks and coppers, is a huge family with about 5,000 species worldwide and 65 in France. The blues in particular can be very abundant, and their presence adds immeasurably to any summer walk in the French countryside. However, apart from a few species they can be hard to identify individually without careful study.

One particularly striking and intriguing group within the blues is the large blues, which are all large (as the name suggests) and belong to the genera *Maculinea* (five species) and *Iolana* (one species). In addition to their size and beauty, they are linked by a curious lifestyle that has only become clear in the last few decades.

The female large blues lay their eggs on their chosen food plant (each species has a different food plant for its eggs), and the tiny caterpillars hatch and start feeding on the food plant. So far, as normal, but after a few weeks the caterpillar ceases feeding on the plant and moves to the ground, where it is rapidly found by ants, which are always of the genus *Myrmica*, and sometimes of a particular species of *Myrmica*.

There is then a more or less complicated series of interactions, resulting in the caterpillar being carried down into the nest of the ants, where it is looked after by them, and its secretions provide food for the ants. In the case of the Large Blue (*Maculinea arion*), Scarce Large Blue (*M. telejus*), and Dusky Large Blue (*M. nausithous*), the growing larva begins feeding on the ant larvae as its primary food, even while the ants continue to protect and lick it. As a result any one ant nest can only support a few butterfly larvae, most commonly just one or two, so these species need extensive populations of ants in order to survive.

In contrast, the two alcon blues (*M. alcon* and *M. rebeli*) feed largely on items brought in by the ants, so a nest is capable of supporting many more caterpillars – up to 20 have been recorded in a single nest. The caterpillars pass the winter in the ants' nest, ceasing their activity at the same time as the ants and pupating in the spring. When the adult butterfly emerges, it pushes its way out of the nest into the fresh air, quite undisturbed by the ants!

This strange and restrictive lifecycle has been only moderately successful recently, because all the large blues have declined considerably. All are in the European Red Data Book for butterflies. Large blues generally favour mountain areas, especially the Pyrenees and southern Alps. One

ABOVE A dense mass of mainly male Escher's Blue butterflies gathered together on a damp stone in the Pyrenees.
BELOW The Marais de Lavours, near Chambéry, a lovely marshland reserve that is home to three species of large blue.

excellent site where three species occur together (the Scarce, Dusky and Alcon) is the Marais de Lavours near Chambéry.

The Nymphalidae family, in its narrow sense excluding the browns, is a major butterfly family both in France and else-

ABOVE A Glanville Fritillary resting on a Common Spotted Orchid during wet weather.

ABOVE The lovely little Knapweed Fritillary has attractively mottled wings on the upper surface.

BELOW A Marsh Fritillary resting on an Early Marsh Orchid. This species has declined significantly over much of its range.

where. Almost all of its species are large, colourful and striking, often powerful fliers and usually very conspicuous. It includes the fritillaries, the admirals, and the common 'vanessids' such as the Red Admiral (*Vanessa atalanta*), Peacock (*Inachis io*) and Small Tortoiseshell (*Aglais urticae*).

One of the most striking species, indeed one of the most striking of all European butterflies, is the Two-tailed Pasha (*Charaxes jasius*), a boldly marked and coloured species, with a wingspan of 7–8 cm and two tails on each hindwing. It only occurs in the south of France, where it is most likely to be seen in late summer gathered around fallen rotten fruit. The larval food plant is the Strawberry Tree, so it is most frequent where this occurs, especially near the coast. This is one of the few French butterflies to have tropical rather than temperate origins, and it is easy to imagine it in the tropics.

Closely related species include the lovely Purple Emperor (*Apatura iris*), with boldly marked purple and white wings, most often seen coming down to the ground to feed on anything damp and unpleasant smelling! One particularly striking and sought-after butterfly in this group is the Camberwell Beauty (*Nymphalis antiopa*), known as the Mourning Cloak in the United States, which has a wingspan of up to 6 cm and deep purplish-black wings boldly edged with a band of creamy yellow that turns white in individuals that have hibernated over winter. Widespread in France, especially in wooded mountain areas, it is very nomadic so its appearances are unpredictable.

Most of the vanessid species are quite simple to identify, each having a distinctive combination of characters. The fritil-

ABOVE The Queen of Spain Fritillary is a highly mobile migrant butterfly that can be found at almost any time of the year except in the coldest months.

BELOW The little Meadow Fritillary is a common but easily overlooked butterfly, as it can be hard to identify.

ABOVE The caterpillars of the Large Tortoiseshell and Camberwell Beauty butterflies feeding on a willow in the Pyrenees.

laries are another matter! There are 33 species in France, all with a broadly similar combination of tawny orange wings more or less boldly marked with black dots or lines on the upper surfaces. To some extent, size helps in identification, as there is a group of very large and distinctive species, including the Silver-washed Fritillary (*Argynnis paphia*), which is widespread throughout France, and the Cardinal (*A. pandora*), which is locally common close to the Mediterranean and southern Atlantic coasts.

This leaves a large group of confusing smaller fritillaries, most of which occur in similar habitats – flowery meadows that are often slightly damp. Unless you are very experienced,

identification usually requires a good look at the underside of the wing as well as the upper surface, followed by a lot of thought and head shaking! Whatever the exact species, their presence adds immeasurably to almost any open, sunny flowery habitat, where they may become very abundant in early to midsummer, especially in hilly areas. Incidentally, all the Nymphalidae share the characteristic of having only four apparent legs instead of six, as the front pair are tiny, furry and tucked away, playing no part in walking.

The final significant butterfly family in France is the Satyridae, the browns, which are closely related to the nymphalids and have the same reduced front legs. As the name suggests, most of the species are brown, and they include the ringlets, the graylings, the browns and the heaths, as well as the boldly black-and-white marbled whites (*Melanargia* spp.).

ABOVE A huge Giant Peacock Moth, with a wingspan of up to 15 cm, resting during the day.
BELOW A close-up view of the boldly marked Convolvulus Hawkmoth, a common migrant nocturnal species.

Moths

Moths are closely related to butterflies – they all belong to the order Lepidoptera – and there are actually many more species of moth than butterfly in France, though they are generally less well known and appreciated. They differ in several ways, though the differences are not always clear-cut. Generally speaking, butterflies fly by day, have antennae with distinct clubs on the ends and have quite separate wings. Moths have a variety of different antenna shapes, though the antennae are rarely clubbed. They mainly fly at night, and most have their hindwings and forewings linked by a sort of hairy hook called a frenulum. Usually moths and butterflies settle at rest in differ-

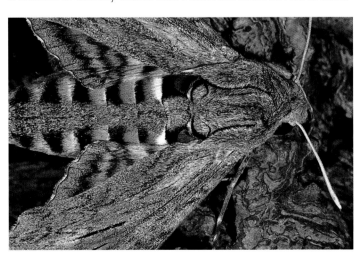

ent ways, too. In many ways, though, the distinction is an academic one.

There are several thousand species of moth in France, making them a real challenge for the naturalist, but a few stand out. There are a number of moths that normally fly during the day (most will fly in the day if disturbed, but are habitually nocturnal), so they tend to get noticed almost as much as butterflies. Some of the most conspicuous are in a couple of related families, the eggars and the emperors.

The Oak Eggar (*Lasiocampa quercus*) is a yellow and brown moth with a wingspan of about 5 cm that flies rapidly over heaths and grasslands. The rather similar Tau Emperor (*Aglia tau*) is larger and has a large blue spot on each wing – it flies vigorously and rapidly in clearings and around the edges of beech woods, and is most active in the morning. These insects look like butterflies, but they fly more rapidly and directly, and usually travel further, giving the impression of being on a mission – in contrast to butterflies, which have a more erratic flight. Male Emperor Moths (*Saturnia pavonia*) fly by day in search of the sedentary females, which emit a scent that the males can detect up to 2 km away! Like many male moths, they have feathery, branched antennae that are incredibly sensitive to just a few molecules of the female scent.

There is a close relative of the Emperor Moth, the Giant Peacock Moth (*Saturnia pyri*), which is Europe's largest moth with a wingspan of up to 15 cm, closer in size to bats and birds than to most moths! It has beautifully marbled, greyish-brown wings with a large eyespot on each wing. Although this species is nocturnal, it is not infrequently seen in the day, often settling around street lights and house lights at night and remaining there through the following day, and it is large enough to be noticed in flight at dusk. It only occurs in the southern half of France. The extraordinary Spanish Moon Moth (*Graellsia isabellae*) is worth mentioning, though it too is mainly nocturnal. Its wings are a lovely pale greenish-blue veined with brown, and its hindwings are extended into two long tails. This rare species occurs in and around conifer woods in the Alps and Pyrenees, though it occasionally comes to light in the higher alpine villages.

Another very significant family of day-flying moths is the burnet and forester moths in the Zygaenidae. All of these are day flying, and they share other characteristics with butterflies, too, in that they are brightly coloured. The burnets also have club-shaped antennae, though the clubs are more paddled-shaped and therefore different from those of butterflies. There are about 30 species of burnet in France, all of which are broadly similar in having bluish-black forewings spotted with red and red hindwings, though there are many variations in the numbers of spots and the extent of the markings. The foresters (*Adscita* spp.) are slender turquoise or greenish species without clubbed antennae, which are often found on dry, flowery grassland.

The hawkmoth family Sphingidae (known as sphinxes in North America) consists mainly of nocturnal species, though a few are day flying. The most frequently seen is the delightful little Hummingbird Hawkmoth (*Macroglossum stellatarum*), which has brownish-grey forewings and orange-red hindwings. It is particularly distinctive because of its behaviour – it is constantly on the move, flicking between flowers and hovering in front of them for a few seconds while drinking nectar with its long proboscis, then moving on. It is remarkably like a tiny hummingbird, for which it is often mistaken. It is a common and widespread resident that overwinters in the south, but migrates northwards right up to far northern Europe and up onto high mountain slopes, wherever there are flowers. It has become more frequent in the north in recent years, probably due to the steady pattern of climate warming.

Two other widespread, though less common diurnal hawk-moths are the Broad-bordered Bee Hawkmoth (*Hemaris fuciformis*) and the Narrow-bordered Bee Hawkmoth (*H. tityus*). They are rather similar, with furry bodies and transparent wings, not unlike large bumblebees, though their flight is more direct and they hover at flowers to feed. They are not major migrants like the Hummingbird Hawkmoth, and are most commonly found in sheltered flowery glades in more wooded areas.

The remaining hawkmoths are mainly nocturnal, and frequently much larger and more impressive than the day-flying ones, though they are less often seen. The two most striking and dramatic species are both regular migrants

ABOVE The Poplar Hawkmoth (*Laothoe populi*) is well camouflaged, looking rather like a cluster of dead leaves when resting.
BELOW A Hummingbird Hawkmoth coming in to feed on a Woolly Thistle, uncoiling its proboscis as it approaches.

northwards from Africa. The Death's Head Hawkmoth (*Acherontia atropos*) is an extraordinary beast, with large, boldly marbled wings, a blue, yellow and black furry body, and a distinctive skull-like design on its thorax – an unmistakeable combination. The larvae feed on potato leaves and various nightshades, but the adults feed frequently on honey,

entering beehives unscathed in order to get it. When handled, they squeak quite loudly. This species regularly turns up in northern France, but is much more common in the south.

The Oleander Hawkmoth (*Daphnis nerii*) is also dramatic, with large green, white and purple marbled wings, and a green-striped body, and is also a migrant, but rarely goes much further north than the Alps. The larvae feed on Oleander (*Nerium oleander*) or occasionally periwinkles (*Vinca* spp.). In all the hawkmoths, the larvae are almost as impressive as the adults – large, often brightly coloured and with a horn at the tail end. In the Spurge Hawkmoth (*Hyles euphorbiae*), the larvae are probably more conspicuous than the adults, and certainly more often seen as they feed openly on spurge (*Euphorbia* spp.) plants.

One quite different moth that is frequently noticed – or at least, one aspect of its lifecycle is often seen – is the Pine Processionary Moth (*Thaumetopoea pityocampa*). The moth itself is inconspicuous – small and greyish-brown in colour – but the larvae live colonially and spin themselves quite sizeable nests among the foliage of conifers, particularly pines, consisting of a mass of silken threads up to 30 cm long. This nest acts as the home base for the caterpillars, which pass the day safe inside it, emerging at night to forage among the leaves, which they eat voraciously.

The nests of the Pine Processionary Moth are very conspicuous and abundant, and the insects are often noticed again when they come to pupate – the larvae leave the nest in a long procession, come down to the ground, then proceed in a long line to a suitable pupation site, where they disperse and pupate at or under the soil level. These long lines of caterpillars are highly visible, and may frequently cross paths, roads (not very successfully) and other obstacles to reach their destination. The front caterpillar leads, but if there is a problem, after a good deal of milling about another leader is 'appointed', and the whole procession starts again!

The famous French naturalist J.H. Fabre undertook various experiments with the caterpillars (and many other insects) in the 19th century, one of which involved placing the caterpillars around the rim of a flowerpot so that they formed a continuous circle. Apparently they continued round and round until they fell off, though they lasted for seven days! The Pine Processionary Moth is a considerable pest in managed woodlands, where it is thought to greatly reduce the productivity of the trees. It is widespread in France and becoming more common in northern regions. There is also a related species on oaks – the Oak Processionary Moth (*T. processionea*), which has similar habits but is less conspicuous and rarely seen.

ABOVE, LEFT The larval nest of the Pine Processionary Moth at dusk, as the larvae begin to emerge for their night's feeding.
BELOW, LEFT The strikingly marked caterpillars of the Spurge Hawkmoth are able to feed openly during the day as they are both distasteful and poisonous to predators.

Dragonflies and Damselflies

After butterflies, dragonflies and damselflies are probably the most popular of insects. Often known as 'birdwatcher's insects' for their attractive combination of large size, strong colours, continuous activity and fascinating behaviour, the Odonata are becoming increasingly popular and well studied. Nowadays, there are also several good field guides to European dragonflies, covering all the French species, which make identification easier.

France is well blessed with dragonflies and damselflies because of its wide latitudinal range and its enormous range of suitable habitats. About 100 species have been recorded, and it is interesting to look at their origins. None is completely endemic to France, though many occur in a quite restricted area, and are endemic, for example, to south-west France and Iberia. Many species, as is the case with the butterflies, occur in several countries to the north of France. These include the Common Hawker (*Aeshna juncea*), the Downy Emerald (*Cordulia aenea*) and many of the damselflies. About a quarter are of primarily Mediterranean distribution, including the Copper Demoiselle (*Calopteryx haemorrhoidalis*), the Lesser Emperor (*Anax parthenope*) – though this is currently spreading northwards, like several other species – and the Tyrrhenian endemic damselfly the Island Bluetail (*Ischnura genei*), which only occurs on Corsica within France.

Ten species are known (within Europe) only from Iberia and adjacent parts of France, including the striking Splendid Cruiser (*Macromia splendens*), which occurs as far north-east as the southern parts of the Massif Central. Finally, there is a group of species whose main area of distribution is within Africa, and France lies at the northern edge of their geographical range. These include the nail-varnish pink Broad Scarlet (*Crocothemis erythraea*) and the attractive plum-coloured Violet Dropwing (*Trithemis annulata*). Both species are common virtually throughout Africa including tropical areas, and are now gradually extending their range northwards.

Among the damselflies (Zygoptera), there are about 33 species in France (and a few more that may or may not occur regularly). They are generally less striking than the dragonflies, smaller, less active and with less actively territorial males. A few stand out, though, and are often noticed. All of the demoiselles are particularly conspicuous by virtue of their large and often coloured wings. In flight, they are sometimes confused with butterflies, though they are clearly distinct when at rest, and the wing colour does not originate from coloured scales as in butterflies.

The male of the Banded Demoiselle (*Calopteryx splendens*) is very distinctive and beautiful, with a wingspan of about 7 cm and a lovely metallic blue abdomen, though its most conspicuous feature, especially when in flight, is the bold blue patch on each of its wings. The species occurs almost throughout France, with the exception of higher mountain areas, nearly

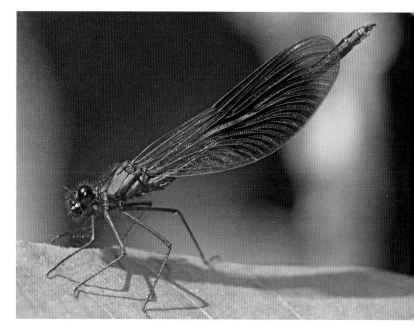

ABOVE A male Banded Demoiselle damselfly resting on a leaf between bouts of territorial activity.

always in small to medium base-rich rivers, avoiding large rivers, still waters and acidic streams on the whole. Where present, it can often be abundant, with clouds of individuals displaying, feeding, mating and loafing along the riverbank – a wonderful sight on a sunny summer day.

The rather similar Western Demoiselle (*C. xanthostoma*) differs in having wings coloured right to the tips (as well as in other details), and is an essentially Iberian species in rather similar habitats throughout south-west France. The Copper Demoiselle (*C. haemorrhoidalis*) has even more highly coloured wings and a coppery red body (in the male), and can

BELOW A male Common Hawker patrolling his territory around a small high mountain lake.

be seen throughout Mediterranean France, most commonly on small shady streams. The final species in the genus is the Beautiful Demoiselle (*C. virgo*), the largest and darkest of the group, with wholly smoky-coloured wings and a greenish-blue body (in the male). It occurs throughout France and in general prefers smaller, more acidic and often shadier running waters; it only rarely overlaps with the other species and is much less warmth demanding.

There are many other species of damselfly, all interesting and attractive, though they are too numerous to mention here. However, there is one other genus that is of special interest as it departs from the usual lifecycle of damselflies, in which the underwater nymph lives for one or more years, but individual adults only live for a month or so. In the winter damselflies (*Sympecma* spp.), the adults mainly emerge in middle to late summer, and feed through the rest of the summer. As the weather cools, they find hibernation sites in hollow trees, among leaves or anywhere protected from cold. They re-emerge in spring (though in warmer areas they can be seen on the wing in almost any month) and commence mating and egg-laying, before gradually dying off over the late spring months, so the mature insects live for about ten months. Much the most common species in France is the Common Winter Damsel (*S. fusca*), which occurs throughout the country (and, interestingly, right on northwards to southern Scandinavia, so it is not heavily affected by winter temperatures despite its hibernation habits).

The remainder of the 100 species of Odonata are dragonflies. These are much more conspicuous than damselflies and therefore familiar to almost everyone. The hawkers (*Aeshna* spp.) are large and highly mobile dragonflies, with aggressive and territorial males in most species and a total body length of 7–8 cm. There are half a dozen or so species in France, all rather similar in appearance, though the Green-eyed or Norfolk Hawker (*A. isosceles*) has a plain tawny-brown body, lacking any blue, and large green eyes, while the impressive Brown Hawker (*A. grandis*) has a dark brown, blue-spotted body and smoky yellowish-brown wings, their colour being obvious even in flight.

The common and widespread Southern or Blue Hawker (*A. cyanea*) is a typical *Aeshna* in appearance, boldly marked with black, green and blue on its abdomen. However, it is unusual in one respect: most of the *Aeshna* species are endophytic – that is, the females lay their eggs in the tissues of submerged aquatic plants for protection – but the Southern Hawker is often seen laying its eggs well out of the water on vegetation, or even on wood or concrete. When the egg hatches into the tiny prolarva, this small, legless creature has to move itself into a position to drop into the water before it can develop as normal. Superficially, this seems like curious behaviour, introducing an additional possible weak link into the lifecycle, but since the Southern Hawker is the most common and widespread hawker in France, it must be doing something right.

The emperors or darners (*Anax* spp.) are wonderful dragonflies, including what is generally considered to be the largest European dragonfly, the Blue Emperor. The males have a striking turquoise-blue abdomen and a green thorax, and fly strongly with a slightly down-curved abdomen. All three species in the genus are of southern or eastern origin, and are currently expanding their range northwards and westwards.

As already mentioned, no species of dragonfly are entirely endemic to France, though there are four species of Iberian or western Mediterranean endemic that occur in France and may have substantial populations there. The intriguingly named Western Spectre (*Boyeria irene*) is a large, pale greyish species that occurs on many rivers throughout south-western France, but it flies quietly and unassumingly, with its main period of activity being around dusk, so it tends to be overlooked. Two of the clubtails are south-west European endemics confined to Iberia and south-west France. The Pronged Clubtail (*Gomphus graslinii*) is a smallish, bright yellow and black dragonfly, not uncommon on rivers in the hillier parts of south-west France, while the Western Clubtail (*G. pulchellus*) is a paler, faded-looking species that occurs almost throughout France on many types of water body, and is slowly spreading northwards.

Grasshoppers and Crickets

The order Orthoptera includes all the grasshoppers and bush-crickets, as well as the true crickets and mole crickets. This is an essentially warmth-loving group that reaches its peak further south. There are at least 600 species in Europe as a whole, but many of these are in the extreme southern countries such as Spain and Greece, and France has fewer than half this total. The grasshoppers are generally rather small diurnal species, with short antennae, vegetarian habits and no blade-like ovipositor, whereas the bush-crickets are often active at night, are omnivorous and have very long, thread-like antennae, and the females usually have a long, dagger-like ovipositor. True crickets are similar, but rather flatter and with broader wings.

The sounds of grasshoppers and crickets are familiar to almost everyone (until the listener reaches a certain age, when they eventually become inaudible), and each species produces a distinctive song, which is often a more reliable means of identification, and certainly of survey estimates, than sight. Grasshoppers produce their songs by rubbing their hindlegs against their forewings, making a buzzing sound that varies according to the speed of movement, the number of acoustic pegs and the rhythm. Bush-crickets, by contrast, produce their

CLOCKWISE FROM THE TOP, LEFT Lesser Emperor dragonfly settled out of the wind; male Violet Dropwing, an African species that has spread into southern France; male Ruddy Darter (*Sympetrum sanguineum*); Common Winter Damsel after overwintering; male Broad Scarlet (*Crocothemis erythraea*), which is common throughout France; Goldenring, or Golden-ringed Dragonfly.

songs by raising their forewings and rubbing them together, and their songs are usually both longer lasting and higher in pitch than those of grasshoppers.

The grasshoppers are rather hard to distinguish without careful examination and some experience, but some groups are more distinctive than others. One group of species specializes in 'flash colouration' as a means of defence against predators. These are rather dull, well-camouflaged species, but if they are disturbed their brightly coloured blue or red hindwings suddenly flash brightly, before disappearing when the insect settles again. The bird or other predator searches for the brightly coloured object, and usually fails to find it – at least, that is the theory.

There are several French species showing this camouflage feature, including the blue-winged *Oedipoda coerulescens*, which is quite widespread, and the slightly larger *Sphingonotus caerulans*. Red-winged species include *Oedipoda germanica* and the dark-coloured *Psophus stridulus*, both of which are widespread in suitable warm, dry habitats. There seems to be no particular difference in behaviour or effect between the two colours, and the different types frequently live in the same habitats.

BELOW A mass of alpine grasshoppers *Gomphocerus sibiricus* in a sheltered hollow at almost 3,000 m in the Vanoise National Park.

One of the largest of the grasshoppers is the Migratory Locust (*Locusta migratoria*), with a body length of up to 6 cm. Its core area is further south than France, and in the north of its range (including France) it normally only occurs in its more greenish solitary phase and never becomes a significant swarming pest as it can in Africa. A similar and equally large species is the Egyptian Grasshopper (*Anacridium aegyptium*), which is browner, non-swarming and has conspicuous vertically striped eyes. It is strongly southern in France, occurring mainly in the Mediterranean departments.

Most of the bush-crickets tend to remain unnoticed, except, perhaps for their background calls at night in the warmer parts of France. One of the most impressive, and one of the largest insects in Europe, is *Saga pedo*, whose French names translate as the Jagged Magician or the Provence Lobster! In Western Europe there are only females, and these can have a body length of 6–7 cm, plus a very long ovipositor – they are fearsome creatures. You may be wondering how the species survives if there are only females. Here, parthenogenesis comes to the rescue. The female lays batches of eggs that develop into adults (females, of course) without fertilization – effectively they are clones of their mother. This impressive insect is rare, and more or less confined to calcareous *garrigue* in the south of France. Another species that is conspicuous enough to merit a common name is the Zizi or Tizi, though the name may also

be applied to the related browner species *Ephippiger terrestris* and *E. provincialis*. These are large bush-crickets with very short wings and a distinctive raised saddle on their backs. The name, of course, comes from their call – a monotonous, frequently repeated '*zi-zi*'.

Some of the most distinctive sounds of the French countryside come from the true crickets in the family Gryllidae. Many flowery meadows, especially those in the mountains and less dry parts of the country, emit a continuous pulsing call that is clearly coming from hundreds of insects. The origin of this wall of sound is the black beetle-like Field Cricket (*Gryllus campestris*), which lives in little burrows in the fields, from where it calls insistently, especially in early summer. A quieter but equally distinctive call is that of the little brown Wood Cricket (*Nemobius sylvestris*), vast numbers of which live in the leaf litter of warm deciduous woodland, especially in clearings or along the edges, producing a wonderful mellifluous purring during much of the summer and autumn. They occur throughout France, but are most common in the south.

Finally, there are the mole-crickets, which are quite closely related though in a different family, the Gryllotalpidae. These are extraordinary large brown insects up to 5 cm long and very stocky with it, and have much of the charm – and structure – of an earth-moving machine. They pass most of their life underground, particularly in damp soil, but the males produce a continuous nightjar-like churring (which is often mistaken for the calls of nightjars if you are close enough to hear it well) from the mouths of their burrows, especially at night. Surprisingly, on warm nights they can also fly in an ungainly fashion. The most common and widespread species is *Gryllotalpa gryllotalpa*, though in southern parts of France there are two closely related species, *G. septemdecimchromosomica* (!), and *G. vineae*.

Beetles

There are an awful lot of beetles in the world, with at least 400,000 species described worldwide and over 20,000 in Western Europe alone. The Scottish geneticist and evolutionary biologist J.B.S. Haldane was once asked what he thought his evolutionary studies had revealed about the nature of God. He famously replied: 'An inordinate fondness for beetles', and you can see what he meant!

Most of the vast number of Western European beetles are inconspicuous, nocturnal or very similar to closely related species, though there are a number of beetles that are of special

TOP, RIGHT An Egyptian Grasshopper, probably the largest of the French grasshoppers.

CENTRE, RIGHT The black, rather beetle-like Field Cricket, briefly out of its burrow.

BOTTOM, RIGHT One of the mole-crickets, showing its long body and powerful legs.

ABOVE A male Stag Beetle on an old tree trunk, preparing to do battle with a rival.
BELOW Rose Chafers, a type of beetle, are a striking bright, shiny, jewel-like green, readily visible when they visit flowers.

interest for one reason or another. The Stag Beetle (*Lucanus cervus*) is an extraordinary creature that is widespread throughout France with the exception of Corsica. The males are huge, at up to 8 cm long one of the largest European beetles, and wield a massive pair of jaws that are very aptly referred to as antlers both for their shape and for their purpose, since male Stag Beetles, like deer, engage in locked-antler battles. The beetle larvae live in dead wood, often oak in pieces that must be large enough to not rot significantly during the four or five years that they spend in this phase. They emerge throughout the summer,

and fly with a rather ungainly flight at dusk. The females are rather smaller, without the 'antlers', and there are related smaller species.

Chafers are abundant in France and there are many species, such as the May Bug or Cockchafer (*Melolontha melolontha*), which is well known for its habit of crashing into lighted windows. However, the most impressive – and one of the most distinctive of European beetles – is the Pine Chafer (*Polyphylla fullo*), which is mainly southern in France, but also occurs all the way up the Atlantic seaboard. It has a boldly patterned black and yellow body of about 4 cm long, with striking broad antennae (in the male); it lives in pines, especially in sandy places, and (unusually among the beetles) the males stridulate loudly. The beetles are attracted by lights at night, so they are quite often seen by campers and other tourists in beach areas with pines. A related group of chafers includes the Rose Chafer (*Cetonia aurata*) and other species in the same genus – not the largest beetles, but ones that are frequently noticed. Adults of both sexes are a bright, sometimes bronzey-green, shiny and jewel-like, and they spend much of their time visiting flowers in the sun.

Glow-worms and fireflies hardly sound like beetles, but they are. The glow-worms, including *Lampyris noctiluca* and the more southerly *Lamprorhiza splendidula*, have a strange life. The females are wingless or short-winged and they sit in warm, grassy places at dusk emitting a soft greenish-blue light from the last three abdomen segments. This is soon detected by the flying males, which look much more like normal beetles. In fact, all stages of the glow-worms' lifecycle emit a certain amount of light, which is produced by the oxidation of a substance called luciferin that gives out a cool and almost heat-free light. Adult glow-worms do not feed much, but the larvae are predators of snails, injecting enzymes into them and reducing them to snail soup.

The closely related fireflies *Luciola lusitanica* have a rather different strategy: the males fly around emitting a regular series of bright flashes, to which the sedentary females respond with their own flashes, and thus the two can happily get together (though in some parts of the world, predators have evolved to emit the same response as the females, pulling in a continuing supply of unsuspecting males).

Fireflies only occur in eastern France, east of the Rhône, and the best place to see them is in the hills of eastern Provence or the lower Maritime Alps, in rough flowery fields. The sight of a whole mass of flashing males on a warm evening is quite extraordinary and magical.

Other Insects

The praying mantis group (order Dictyoptera) is quite well represented in France, though it is essentially a tropical group that is always most common to the south. The distinctive European Mantis (*Mantis religiosa*), known colloquially as the praying mantis, can be up to 7 cm long (females) and is usually bright green, so it is quite conspicuous. Though most common in the south, it occurs well up towards northern France, especially along the coast, and may be very abundant. *Iris oratoria* is rather similar, but has rainbow-coloured hindwings that are used in displays. There is a related but much more southerly Mediterranean species, *Empusa pennata*, which has a long crest on its head. The large nymphs have the look of alien invaders with their long, thin legs, crested thin head and raised, jagged abdomen.

Every visitor to southern France in the summer knows about cicadas, and their French name – *cigales* – crops up regularly in the names of restaurants and other establishments. They are not often seen, but their calls are an almost continuous feature of well-vegetated, warm southern areas. The insects produce these calls by vibrating small membranes on either side of the body, giving a much more continuous sound (in which the pulses are almost indistinguishable) than is the case in crickets. There are actually several species of cicada, all of which have a southerly bias, and the largest is *Tibicen plebejus*. This species feeds mainly in pines and is relatively easily found because of its large size and insistent noise. There are another half dozen or so species, including one that has only recently been separated as a distinct species, on the basis of its song – *Cicada cantilatrix*.

If you spend much time looking for butterflies or orchids in warm flowery grasslands in the southern half of France, you will soon come across some distinctive insects that are hard to classify at first. They resemble dragonflies, but have nothing to do with water, and their antennae are long with knobs on the ends, like small knitting needles. These insects are the ascalaphids, close relatives of the antlions and lacewings in the order Neuroptera.

The most common species in France is *Libelloides longicornis*, which has clear wings, boldly marked with black and veined with gold, though several other species occur. It is an active and skilful aerial predator, flying rapidly in search of prey when the sun is out and settling quickly if the light levels drop. Its eyes are said to be almost exclusively sensitive to ultraviolet radiation.

TOP, RIGHT The male firefly is inconspicuous during the day when he is not sending out his light signals.

CENTRE, RIGHT The female praying mantis is a distinctive insect up to about 7cm long and bright green in colour.

BOTTOM, RIGHT One of the distinctive ascalaphids, *Libelloides coccajus*, warming up just after dawn.

ABOVE The boldly marked male Ladybird Spider is common in stony areas in southern France.

Spiders

Besides all the insect invertebrates, there are numerous other animals without backbones. Probably the most conspicuous and widespread are the spiders, in the class Arachnida. While not as diverse as the insects, spiders are still very varied, with about 750 species in northern Europe and many more further south. They range from tiny, inconspicuous species to large, boldly coloured ones like the Wasp Spider (*Argiope bruenichi*), which can measure as much as 6 cm from leg-tip to leg-tip. In spiders it is almost always the females that are seen, the males being smaller, duller and often shorter-lived.

The female Wasp Spider is a dramatic beast, with a boldly banded yellow and black abdomen, and she sits on an enormous orb-web that is decorated with a zigzag line of silk known as the stabilimentum. This is presumed to be an additional strengthening feature, or possibly a way of preventing birds from flying into the web. The Wasp Spider is widespread in France in sheltered, well-vegetated areas, and is steadily spreading northwards. A close relative, *A. lobata*, occurs only in the south.

The orb-web spiders (*Araneus* spp.) build similar orb-shaped webs, but without the stabilimentum. The most common species is probably the Garden Spider (*A. diadematus*), which occurs everywhere and has a round brown body with a large white cross on the back. A similar but even larger species, *Araneus grossus*, occurs only in the south of France – a fully grown female is the heaviest of all the French spiders.

At the other end of the scale, one of the most appealing of French spiders is the little Ladybird Spider (*Eresus niger*). The females are velvety black and usually remain in a cocoon, but the males are free roaming, with a black thorax, striped legs and a bright red abdomen with four black spots. This species is rare in the north, but becomes increasingly common southwards in *garrigue* and heathy areas.

GALLS ON PLANTS

Almost all species of plant occasionally produce abnormal growths, often in bizarre and conspicuous shapes quite unlike the normal pattern of growth. These are plant galls, caused by an abnormal increase in the size or number of cells as a result of invasion by some external parasite.

Plant galls include familiar species such as the Robin's Pincushion or Bedeguar Gall (*Diplolepis rosae*), the Oak Apple (*Biorhiza pallida*) and the Knopper Gall (*Andricus quercuscalicis*), which replaces acorns on oak trees. All these galls are distinctive enough to be describable and to have common names, yet they are actually atypical parts of their host plant, caused by an invading insect, mite or other organism (the species is indicated here by the scientific name after the common name).

Common causers of small galls are the gall midges (flies of the order Diptera), such as *Jaapiella veronicae*, which causes all the buds of the Germander Speedwell (*Veronica chamaedrys*) to become large and furry.

Many of the most noticeable galls are caused by the gall wasps (Cynipidae), which are part of the enormous Hymenoptera order. They include the Bedeguar Gall, which appears as round, reddish, feathery balls on rose plants, the Marble Gall (*Andricus kollari*), the hard, brown, spherical gall found on young oaks, and the Cherry Gall (*Cynips quercusfolii*), which occurs as hard, cherry-red spheres on the undersides of oak leaves.

In fact, the gall wasps have rather complicated lifecycles. Many of them have two quite different generations per year, in one of which both sexes occur, while in the other only parthenogenetic females occur. To complicate matters further, every generation often produces a quite different gall, each of which was originally thought to have been caused by different species. For example, *Neuroterus quercusbaccarum* produces the Common Spangle Galls that are frequent on the undersides of oaks in autumn. The galls fall off and overwinter, then parthenogenetic females emerge in early spring to lay their eggs in oak buds. These then produce Currant Galls – just like a string of redcurrants – in place of the male oak catkin, from which both males and females later emerge.

One of the most striking galls to be seen in southern France is actually caused by the aphid *Baizonga pistaciae*. Its eggs are laid on the buds of Terebinth Trees (*Pistacia terebinthus*) and relatives; here they give rise to huge, pinkish-red, candle-like structures up to 15 cm long, at the tops of the bushes. The aphids pass the summer in these, then emerge and overwinter underground.

ABOVE The hard Marble Galls on the twigs of a young oak tree in late winter.

ABOVE These unusual horn-like galls on the Terebinth Tree are up to 15 cm long and are caused by a little aphid.

ABOVE Currant Galls, looking very like redcurrants, on the flowers of an oak tree.

ABOVE The Robin's Pincushion or Bedeguar Gall on rose leaves, caused by a gall wasp.

Chapter 9

NATURE CONSERVATION IN FRANCE

Every developed country in the world faces the same problem: how to balance the demands of development and accumulation of wealth with the need to conserve the best in landscape and nature in the country. As a general rule (with a few notable exceptions), the more a country has in terms of its natural assets of biodiversity and habitats, the less effort and emphasis is placed on their protection. The adage that 'you only know what you've got when it's gone' applies as much to nature conservation as to anything. Up until the 1960s, France was conspicuously in the camp of placing little effort into nature conservation: it had no national parks, few statutory reserves, no adequate system of identifying the areas or species that were in need of protection and little official enthusiasm for nature conservation, yet a tremendous wealth of nature was able to survive.

LEFT Autumn view of the extraordinary Gorge du Verdon, one of the many fine sites partly protected by Regional Natural Park status.

In the last few decades, much has changed as France has become aware, both at official and public level, of how special its nature is and how much needs to be done to protect it. It is hardly a time for complacency, and there are still many inadequacies and failures in the system, but there have been vast moves forwards. Any country that is a member of the European Union has to comply with certain European-level requirements, with regard to nature conservation as in other things, in addition to international obligations and country requirements. It is thus hardly surprising that nature conservation in France is a complex business, operating at many levels.

At the state level, there are Réserves Naturelles Nationales (RNN), protecting nationally important sites or species, and generally run by the state. At regional level – as part of the same system – there are now Réserves Naturelles Régionales (RNR), which replaced earlier voluntary reserves. Collectively, RNNs and RNRs cover about 2,500 sq km of French country-side and sea.

In addition, there are reserves run by state organizations such as the Office Nationale de Chasse et Faune Sauvage (ONCFS), which have a different slant on things, but include some important reserves within their small number. The Lac du

Der-Chantecocq is one of their reserves, and there are several other equally large sites spread around France. The state is also involved in the Protected Species legislation, under which numerous species of plant and animal are listed as being protected at one level or another. Though welcome, Protected Species legislation has many weaknesses, notably enforcement and identification, and it is often all too obviously failing to work as sites for rare protected species such as the Aveyron Bee Orchid continue to disappear.

There is an important organization that is principally state funded though separate from the state in other ways, which seeks to protect the coast of France, largely by purchase of land. This is the Conservatoire du Littoral, which currently owns or manages 1,130 sq km of land, covering 900 km of shoreline in 400 sites, and it has often been able to step in at short notice – due to its streamlined administration process – to protect threatened sites. Its current budget allows about 30 million euros per year for land acquisition, and it continues to play an important part in conservation in France.

The state is also involved, of course, in the creation and administration of National Parks, which play a key role in the protection of France's countryside and species. The first two –

The Regional Natural Parks of France

Key
Main roads
High speed railways
International airports
Regional Natural Parks

Vanoise and Port-Crôs – were designated in 1963, and since then the Cévennes, Mercantour, Ecrins and Pyrenees have been added. These are all fabulous areas, now satisfactorily protected and managed, although the total area that they cover is quite small and strongly skewed towards the mountains.

In addition, there is an extensive network of regional parks, or Parcs Naturels Régionaux (PNR), throughout France, covering a very large proportion of the country's land area in 43 parks, stretching from Corsica and the Catalan Pyrenees, northwards to Armorique in Brittany and the Caps et Maries d'Opale near Calais (see map, page 159). The largest are immense – for example, the Volcans d'Auvergne covers 3,950 sq km, the Grandes Causses 3,150 sq km and the Ballons des Vosges about 3,000 sq km. They are spread throughout France, so their coverage is considerable. Their role in the conservation of nature is much less easy to assess, partly because they vary in their aims and abilities, but also because they do not start out with a protective function, but rather have the aim of maintaining traditional ways of life and landscape within the designated areas. Sometimes this involves the conservation of nature somewhere within the park, though often it may not.

In many countries, such as Britain, the Netherlands, the USA and Germany, the voluntary sector plays a huge role in conservation of the countryside and nature. In France, this is not the case. This is partly due to different attitudes towards conservation, and less of a perceived need, due to the wealth of habitats that France still has, but it may also be part of a higher expectation among French people that the government should take care of such problems. French people expect – and pay for – very high levels of state services, and nature conservation falls under this general heading.

The major French bird conservation charity is the Ligue pour la Protection des Oiseaux (LPO) and it currently has 43,500 members. By contrast, the Royal Society for the Protection of Birds (RSPB), the UK equivalent, has over one million members and a very strong voice in planning and lobbying, as well as over a hundred reserves. In addition, there are over three million members of the National Trust (which includes many nature and countryside conservation aims within its portfolio), and the association of County Wildlife Trusts counts about 750,000 members split between the various counties. These represent a very considerable voice influencing decisions, as well as a large body of manpower and a substantial amount of money for land purchase, which barely exists in France at the moment.

It is obvious that France still has a wonderfully attractive countryside that continues to be rich in species. Forest management, traditional transhumance, hunting and the maintaining of a traditional form of agriculture (with the help of EU subsidies) all play a significant part in keeping this lovely countryside as a rich and diverse place, and there is much to admire in this process and much to be proud of. There is a problem, however, in that France needs to put more into identifying the sites and habitats that must be protected if a balance is to be struck, and then to devise and implement policies to protect them. Too many habitats – such as sand dunes, marshes, fens, lowland flowery grasslands and heaths – can easily fall through the current net, and marvellously biodiverse sites can simply disappear overnight under the present regime before anyone has realized that this has happened.

Sites of Special Interest and Value

1. Les Sept-Iles The premier seabird site in France, with at least 12 breeding species, lying just off the north Brittany coast a few kilometres north-west of Perros-Guirec.

2. Golfe du Morbihan and Quiberon Peninsula Immediately west of Vannes, there is a huge tidal bay dotted with islands that is visited by internationally important numbers of waders and waterfowl in winter and at passage periods. The Quiberon Peninsula, which juts out south-westwards, has huge areas of dunes and other habitats, some protected as reserves.

3. Grand Brière Marshes A vast area of low-lying marshland, pastures and open water just to the north of Nantes and the Loire estuary, and wholly within the Grand Brière PNR. It is one of the best wetlands in France, particularly good for breeding birds, amphibians, dragonflies and wetland plants.

BELOW Mixed intertidal habitats in the enormous Golfe du Morbihan, in Brittany.

ABOVE Pollarded Ash trees and duckweed-filled ditch in Marais Poitevin PNR.

4. Baie de Bourgneuf and the Ile de Normoutier This lies south of Nantes and north-west of Challans. It is an enormous intertidal and coastal area, which covers at least 50,000 ha, and is particularly important for wintering waders and waterfowl, although there is much else of interest to see in the surrounding coastal habitats.

5. Marais de Poitevin This is an enormous area of low-lying coastal marshes and associated habitats between Niort and the Atlantic, all of which lie within the Marais Poitevin PNR. Although much of the area is under agricultural use, which is often quite intensive, there are in addition excellent examples of grazed coastal marshes, dunes, mudflats and salt marshes, as well as open waters, supporting an extremely wide variety of species.

6. Baie de Veys Extensive mudflats, salt marshes and associated habitats, at the south-east point of the Cherbourg Peninsula. Internationally important for wintering and passage birds. Part nature reserve, and wholly within the Marais du Cotentin et du Bessin PNR.

7. Somme Estuary An important area for wintering, passage and breeding birds, with good access provided by the Marquenterre Ornithological Park.

8. Baie du Mont St Michel Over 60,000 ha of intertidal habitats of international importance for wintering and migrating birds at the south-western edge of the Cherbourg Peninsula.

9. The Brenne A fascinating and important wetland area lying between Châteauroux and Châtellerault, in the Indre department. It contains more than 1,400 lakes, and collectively they support an enormous range of wetland species from all groups. It lies wholly within La Brenne PNR.

10. Fontainebleau Forest One of the largest and most varied of *forêts domaniales* lying immediately south of Paris. It is managed more for recreation and conservation than for timber, and has a fine range of breeding woodland birds, butterflies, beetles, flowers and much else, with good visitor facilities and easy access.

11. Lac du Der-Chantecocq Large, important lake lying southwest of St Dizier, well known for huge numbers of Common Cranes, but also of great interest for many other reasons.

12. Compiègne Forest A large ancient *forêt domaniale* adjacent to Compiègne, about 70 km east of Paris, particularly good for breeding birds such as woodpeckers, and a rich flora.

13. Ballons des Vosges PNR The high southern parts of the Vosges Mountains lie within this park west of Colmar and Mulhouse, and it is probably the best area in which to appreciate the forests and high montane grasslands of these mountains. It also contains some of the best bogs and moorlands in France, with a wide range of species.

14. High Jura North-west of Geneva (though wholly within France) lies the highest part of the Jura Mountains, with a marvellous mixture of woodlands, high montane grasslands and wetlands, notably rich in flowers and butterflies, especially around Crêt de la Neige and Crêt Pela. It all lies within the Haut Jura PNR, and part lies within a large nature reserve.

15. Basin d'Arcachon A large, enclosed bay on the coast just south-west of Bordeaux, with extensive mudflats, salt marshes and nearby dunes. This is one of the best places to see a range of south-west coastal species and habitats, with the highest dunes in Europe at Pilat, a good offshore seabird colony (Banc d'Arguin) and a very accessible bird reserve at Teich.

ABOVE The beautiful wooded upper Loue Valley, which is located in the Jura Mountains.

16. Etang de Cousseau Although quite small, this nature reserve close to the coast north-west of Bordeaux, just north of Lacanau, is a good microcosm of the extensive dune habitats that can be found all along this *Landes* coast, containing dune slacks, a large lake, marshland, forest and open dunes, all rich in species.

17. Forêt de Grésigne A beautiful large state forest overlying limestone, to the east of Montauban, north-west of Castelnau-de-Montmiral. It is predominantly deciduous and contains many areas of scrub and open grassland, as well as being enormously rich in insects, birds and flowers – for example, it is considered to be the third best site in Europe for beetles, and has 20 species of bats.

18. Plateau de Millevaches An extensive upland plateau lying at about 1,000m, situated east of Limoges and north-west of Usse. Although the interest is rather diffuse, this area contains some excellent examples of high-rainfall bogs, moorland and woodland, as such representing the wetter western slopes of the Massif Central.

19. Volcans d'Auvergne PNR Southwards from Clermont-Ferrand, over an enormous area, lies the best area of volcanic mountain scenery in France, containing many fine lakes, grasslands and woodlands, rising to over 1,800 m in places. The flora and fauna are a fascinating mixture of southern, northern, lowland, mountain and endemics.

20. The *Causses* Lying roughly between Millau, Mende and Alès, the *causses* are a fascinating area of high limestone plateaux, dissected by deep gorges such as the Gorge du Tarn. Much of the area is unspoiled, with very extensive, open flow-ery grassland rich in special species including endemics. Part of the area lies in the Grand Causses PNR, and part within the Cévennes National Park.

21. Marais de Lavours Reserve Although it is not especially large (about 500 ha) this reserve, which is located at the north-western point of Lac du Bourget, north of Chambéry, is by far the best-protected example of the wetland habitats that have resulted from the gradual infilling of glacial lakes in the pre-alpine areas. It is home to a rich flora and fauna, including three species of large blue butterfly.

ABOVE A large flock of sheep grazing the high pastures of the Vanoise National Park.

sented. Almost 2,000 species of flower occur here, as well as 140 butterfly species and many other rare and interesting animals.

27. Massif des Bauges A beautiful region of pre-alpine mountains, with large areas of beech and other forests, and some wonderful montane grasslands. It lies wholly within the Massif des Bauges PNR.

28. Vercors Mountains One of the most spectacular mountain ranges in France, sited southwards from Grenoble towards Die, with dramatic limestone peaks, cliffs and gorges. The flora of the region is exceptional, particularly when it comes to orchids, in the huge spread of wild habitats to be found here. The whole area lies within the Vercors PNR, and much of it is within a huge protected nature reserve.

22. Les Dombes An extensive area of lakes spread over a large plain centred on the town of Villar-les-Dombes, north-east of Lyon. It is rather similar to the Brenne, with many interesting wetland plants and animals, especially birds.

23. Queyras Valley A quiet microcosm of the Alps, lying south-east of Briançon, up to the Italian border, with many peaks over 3,000m. The flora is exceptionally rich, and it is a valuable area for birds, butterflies and other groups. The whole area lies within the Queyras PNR. The nearby Col d'Izoard is a fine place to appreciate a cross-section of alpine habitats.

24. Mercantour National Park This location includes many of the highest parts of the Maritime Alps between Barcelonette and Nice. The flora and fauna are exceptional, and include many rarities and endemics in all groups. There is good access to the high areas from road passes such as the Col d'Allos and Col de Restefonde.

25. Vanoise National Park France's first National Park, located between Bourg St Maurice and Modane, is a wonderful area of high mountains reaching 3,852 m at its highest point, and protecting a full suite of alpine habitats. Its alpine mammals are particularly notable, though it is rich in all groups.

26. Ecrins National Park A very large and dramatic National Park west of Briançon, with a core area of 918 sq km and a maximum altitude of over 4,000 m, and glaciers, high grasslands, lakes, forests, bogs and many other habitats well repre-

29. Pyrenees National Park This spreads over about 100 km of the high Pyrenees on the Spanish border, centred on the Gavarnie area. Although this is a tightly drawn area, confined only to the highest peaks, it protects the best of this high Pyrenees region, with wonderful examples of cirques, cliffs, peaks and all the montane habitats. The flora and fauna are exceptionally rich, with a vast number of species from all groups, including many Pyrenean endemics.

30. Forêt des Fanges Situated south-east of Quillan, this is a beautiful example of a *forêt domaniale*. It is located over a mid-altitude range of limestone hills, and encompasses a variety of habitats ranging from deciduous woodland to rocky outcrops and flowery grassland. It is a particularly good region for flowers and butterflies.

31. Gorge du Verdon Located south-west of Castellane, this is a fabulous example of an extremely deep limestone gorge, surrounded by high mountains reaching to over 2,000 m in height. It is particularly good for flowers, especially chasmophytes, and there are large populations of cliff-dwelling birds such as Crag Martins (*Ptyonoprogne rupestris*), choughs and Alpine Swifts (*Apus melba*).

32. Camargue Arguably France's best wetland site, with a wonderful range of wetland and coastal habitats grouped around the Rhône delta south of Arles. It is particularly important for birds at all times of the year, but also rich in flowers, reptiles,

OPPOSITE A beautiful unspoiled flowery hay meadow located high in the Vercors Mountains.

ABOVE The extraordinary flat, open and stony steppe-like pastures of the Crau Plain.

amphibians, fish and insects. The whole area lies within the Camargue PNR, and there are more fully protected reserves within this park.

33. Crau Plain East of the Camargue there is a curious area of dry, steppe-like habitat (though now sadly much reduced through encroachment by development and agriculture) quite unlike anywhere else in France. It has many special birds, reptiles, insects and flowers, with specialities such as the Little Bustard, Pin-tailed Sand Grouse and Ocellated Lizard.

34. Cerbère-Banyuls Marine Nature Reserve France's first marine reserve, lying off the shore southwards from Banyuls-sur-Mer to the Spanish border. The sea is very clean here and there is a rich marine life. The information centre in Banyuls can provide more information on visiting.

35. Les Alpilles A sharply defined range of limestone hills just north-east of Arles, with good areas of *maquis* and *garrigue* and

a range of interesting breeding birds including Eagle Owls, Short-toed Eagles and Alpine Swifts.

36. Port-Cros National Park A tiny island National Park lying offshore south of Le Lavandou, which is notable for its undisturbed evergreen forest, interesting reptiles and amphibians, and breeding and visiting seabirds. The surrounding sea is clean and highly diverse with, for example, almost 200 species of fish recorded here.

37. Massif des Maures An interesting and attractive range of wooded hills, rising to 779 m, lying to the north-east of Toulon. Unlike most Provencal mountains, these are made up of acidic impermeable rock, giving them a quite different character as well as a different flora and fauna. They are now the only place to easily see wild tortoises in mainland France.

38. Etang de Biguglia A large brackish to freshwater lagoon lying south of Bastia, partly protected as a nature reserve. It is an important area for both wintering and breeding birds, as well as dragonflies and amphibians such as the endemic Tyrrhenian Tree Frog.

ABOVE The striking white limestone cliffs at Bonifacio close to the southern tip of Corsica.

39. Corsica: the Southern Tip The southernmost part of Corsica, from Bonifacio southwards and including the offshore islands, is quite different from the rest of Corsica. The flora on the limestone is rich, the offshore islands have strong seabird colonies and big areas of sea are protected as a marine reserve.

40. Corsican Mountains The heart of Corsica is a wild and mountainous region rising to 2,706 m at Monte Cinto, and clad in ancient Corsican Pine forest. It is home to many of Corsica's special plants and animals, including the Corsican Nuthatch. Particularly good areas include the Asco Valley, the Spelunca Gorge and the Col de Bavella.

41. Pelagos Cetacean Sanctuary This is a huge voluntary reserve lying in the Ligurian Sea between Corsica, Italy and south-east France. It was established to improve the chances of populations of cetaceans and other marine animals increasing. Boat trips into the area are possible from a variety of ports such as Toulon and St Raphaël.

Further Reading

Guides Gallimard of Paris produce a series of multi-author guides on the Natural Parks (Les Parcs Naturels Regionaux), National Parks (Les Parcs Nationaux) and others of interest.

IGN produce most of the topographical maps covering France, as well as interesting speciality maps such as one depicting the geological curiosities and geology of France. Their website is: www.ign.fr

Abbs, B., *Gardens of France*, Quiller Press, 1994 (London).

Bernard, C., *Fleurs des Causses*, Editions du Rouergue, 1997.

Blondel, J. and Aronson, J., *Biology and Wildlife of the Mediterranean Region*, Oxford University Press, 1999 (Oxford).

Boucher, C., *La flore des Alpes de Haute-Provence*, Edisud, 1998 (Aix-en-Provence).

Cadiou, B. *et al.*, *Oiseaux marins nicheurs de France Metropolitaine*, Editions Biotope, 2004 (Mèze).

Crozier, J., *A Birdwatching Guide to France South of the Loire*, Arlequin Press, 2000 (Chelmsford).

Crozier, J.A., *A Birdwatching Guide to the Pyrenees*, Arlequin Press, 1998 (Chelmsford).

Delforce, P., *The Nature Parks of France*, Windrush Press, 1995 (Gloucestershire).

Dupias, G., *Fleurs du Parc National des Pyrenees* (2 volumes), Parc National des Pyrenees, 1990 (Tarbes).

Gamisans, J., *La flore endémique de la Corse (Corsica)*, Edisud, 1996 (Aix-en-Provence).

Gibbons, Bob, *Travellers' Nature Guide: France*, Oxford University Press, 2003 (Oxford).

Heath, M. and Evans, M. (eds), *Important Bird Areas in Europe, Vol 2: Southern Europe*, Birdlife International, 2000 (Cambridge).

Jestin, P., *Flore du Parc National des Cévennes*, Editions du Rouergue, 1998.

Lebreton, P. *et al.*, *Guide du Naturaliste en Dombes*, Delachaux & Niestle, 1991 (Paris). (One of a series of naturalist-guides covering many areas of France.)

Molina, J., *Flore de Camargue*, PNR de Camargue, 1996 (Arles).

Mosse, F., *À la découverte des réserves naturelles de France*, Nathan/RNF, 1996 (Paris).

Williams, Tony (translator), *Where to Watch Birds in France*, Christopher Helm/LPO, 1992 (London).

Useful Contacts

http://www.societeherpetologiquedefrance.asso.fr/
The national society for the study of reptiles and amphibians.

http://www.lpo.fr
France's premier bird protection society.

http://www.herpfrance.com/
A useful site with information on France's reptiles and amphibians.

http://www.indrenature.net
A good example of a local nature society.

http://sympetrum.free.fr/
For dragonflies and damselflies.

http://www.villagetortues.com/
Address for the tortoise village in the Massif des Maures.

http://www.cigogne-loutre.com
Interesting White Stork and otter site in Alsace.

http://www.maisondesloups.com
A park specializing in wolves.

http://www.parc-animalier-pyrenees.com
One of the more interesting of animal parks.

http://champagne-ardenne.lpo.fr/grues/ferme_aux_grues.htm
An excellent site for watching cranes.

http://www.conservatoire-du-littoral.fr
Important organization concerned with the protection of the coast of France.

http://www.micropolis-insectworld.com/micropolis_uk/index_uk.html
Fascinating entomological centre.

http://www.mnhn.fr/
The Museum of Natural History in Paris.

http://www.parcs-naturels-regionaux.tm.fr/fr/accueil/
The central site for information on France's Natural Regional Parks.

http://natura2000.environnement.gouv.fr/sites
For information on the Natura 2000 sites in France.

http://www.onf.fr
The website of the government forestry department, ONF.

http://www.oceanopolis.com/uk/visite_eng.htm
A good example of a marine aquarium.

http://www.parcsnationaux-fr.com/accueil/
The central site for information on National Parks in France.

http://www.snpn.com/
The national nature protection society.

http://bretagnevivante.asso.free.fr/
Société pour l'Etude et la protection de la nature en Bretagne – perhaps the most effective of the local nature conservation organizations.

http://www.sfepm.org/index.htm
The main society for the study of mammals in France.

http://www.mycofrance.com/
The main society for the study of fungi in France.

http://www.parc-ornithologique-du-teich.com/english/accueil.htm
One of the best of the combined reserves and Ornithological Parks, with excellent viewing facilities.

http://www.reserves-naturelles.org/
The site for official French Nature Reserves.

http://www.ign.fr
The best site for topographical and specialist maps.

Index

Page numbers in **bold** indicate illustrations.

Picture Credits

Robert Dickson/Natural Image 103, bottom.

Daniel Heuclin/NHPA 176.

Mike Lane/Natural Image 10, top, left; 32, bottom; 97, top, centre.

Mike Reid 96.

Peter Wilson/Natural Image 30, top; 50, centre; 50, bottom; 69, right; 97, top, left; 102, top, right; 107, top; 112; 130, top, left; 139, bottom; 140, top, left; 144, top; 145, bottom; 152, top; 155, bottom, left.

Acknowledgements

So many people have helped me in numerous ways with this book – the groups of naturalists that I take to France, who are constantly finding new things or seeing things in new ways; the staff of many nature reserve and national park information offices in France, not to mention the gendarme who came to see why I was parked on a roadside, but ended up telling me where to find the Lady's Slipper Orchid nearby! More specifically, Paul Toynton read the whole text and made a large number of helpful comments, as did Libby whose love and support I value above everything.

This book is dedicated to the memory of my old friend Peter Wilson, who accompanied me on many trips and was always a source of inspiration and information, but who died tragically young in the spring of 2008.